Table of Contents

MW00917418

PRELUDE

Letting go of Mr. Wrong

When you know your worth letting go of Mr. Wrong is easy. However, until a woman knows her worth she will put up with Mr. Wrong. Mr. Wrong usually has a lot of the qualities a woman is looking for in a man such as confidence, charm, good sex and a masculine personality. One thing about Mr. Wrong is that he never gives a woman 100% of himself, and this leaves a woman wanting more. If Mr. Wrong is giving a woman 60% she will spend months or years trying to get the other 40% from him. A woman should realize that a man that isn't giving her 100% doesn't plan on keeping her around or fully committing to her or the relationship. Realize that if a man isn't giving himself to you it's because he doesn't want to, and you can't make a man do something that he doesn't want to do. In fact, the more pressure and demands you place on him the more he'll rebel against you. Mr. Wrong doesn't give you his all because he doesn't want to or because you're not what he wants. Most women are nurturers, and they think that taking care of a man emotionally, sexually, financially, and always being there for him will eventually make him act right or fall in love with them. However, Mr. Wrong never acts right for long. If he does change it will be temporary, and he'll soon revert back to his same old tricks. Usually, Mr. Wrong acts right just to get back on a woman's good side, but as soon as his foot is back in the door, and he's out of the dog house he acts up again. Once a woman realizes her worth she leaves Mr. Wrong because she knows she deserves more than what he's offering her. She refuses to settle for scraps and bones because she wants the full course meal. Her love of herself and her life is more important than holding onto a man that isn't treating her right. This guide will go over the different types of Mr. Wrongs, and how to let go of them. In order to let go, you must realize your self-worth, and this guide will help you with that as well.

This is an all in one guide for women

1. **Help you realize your Self-worth**
2. **How to let go of Mr. Wrong**
3. **Types of Mr. Wrongs**
4. **How to Avoid Getting Played**
5. **Best Player Signs List**
6. **Raise your Self-Esteem**
7. **Raise your Self-Confidence**
8. **Motivate you to better your life**
9. **Facts about men**
10. **Prepare you for Modern Day Dating**

This guide has the ability to help you, but in order for it to help you, you have to take it seriously. Before you go to Chapter one make sure you have a pen and paper. Preferably a journal, notebook or diary.

Dating has changed

Over the years dating has changed. These days more and more men aren't being the gentlemen that they should be. The reason why things have changed is that some women are now playing the role that men should play. Since I'm constantly being asked for advice from women and men I hear firsthand accounts of what's going on in the dating world. Nowadays women are chasing after men when it should be the other way around. Why are they chasing after a man? Men are supposed to be the hunter. In fact, most men love to hunt, and when you chase them you take away the part of dating that makes them feel like a man. However, since more and more women are beginning to do all of the work more and more men are beginning to sit back, and let a woman play their role. These days most men don't have to chase a woman, all they have to do is relax and let a woman do all of the work. Some women are driving miles away to see a guy on the first date. Taking an airplane to another state or country to see a guy they've just met on the Internet. Paying for the first date, begging men for sex, and throwing themselves at a guy just because he's hot. Some women are giving men everything they've got from money to sex without a commitment, and then they wonder why most men aren't looking for a relationship? In the old days, men had to commit, and woo women just to have a chance with them. They would drive miles just to see the woman they were interested in, and they would chase after the woman they were interested in. Nowadays, a lot of men expect women to do all of the work while they relax. If this role reversal keeps up more and more men are going to give up on relationships altogether. I mean why they should be in a relationship when they're already getting everything that they want without being in one? Ladies stop playing a man's role. Let him chase you, and sweep you off your feet. If you're doing all the calling, texting, planning and chasing you're doing what a man is supposed to do. It's okay to call him first sometimes, but if you're doing it first all the time you are chasing after him. Realize that a man is more interested in a woman that makes him feel like a man, not a woman that is throwing herself at him, and chasing him like she's a man too. Whatever happened to letting the dog chase the cat? Nowadays the cat is chasing after the dog. Make him chase after you, and put some effort into getting you. Then when he catches you he'll know that you're a prize worth keeping. If a guy isn't chasing after you, he's not interested in you, and you need to let him go. If he never calls you first you're not a priority to him, and you need to let him go. Unless women stop making it easy for men, most men won't feel a need to commit. Most of the women that have contacted me have asked me questions about their friends with benefits that don't want to commit to them. Well, ever since friends with benefits became popular more and more men are wanting that type of relationship. That type of relationship is perfect for men because they can have everything they want from a woman with no strings attached. Women need to stop settling for friends with benefits and bring back commitment. Stop letting men keep you around just for sex, and start making men step up to the plate. I'm not saying that the old days were perfect, but I am saying that the women in the old days demanded more respect from men than modern women do, and they definitely didn't chase after men. Back then men talked to a woman's father before he approached her, took her on sweet dates, and swept her off her feet just to be with her. Now, all a man has to do is go to the club, buy a girl a few drinks, and he gets to take her home. Are a few drinks all it takes for him to get you in bed? Now, all a man has to do is take a girl on a first date at some 20-dollar restaurant then take her home to his bed. Is a 20-dollar dinner all it takes to get you into bed? These days a man can have a woman drive miles just to see him, but back in the day he would have had to drive miles to see her, and he would be happy to do it. Starting today look for a man that will be the man, and stop chasing after a man that isn't putting any effort into getting you or keeping you.

Are you doing what a man is supposed to be doing? If so, you need to stop it because the more you do it the less he'll do it. If you want him to be the man of the house you need to let him take charge, and act like the man. From now on if a man isn't chasing you, move on, because he is Mr. Wrong.

Table of Contents

Chapter 1. MR. WRONG

The wrong person gives you 50% of themselves, but you hold onto them because you think they'll eventually give you the 50% that's missing.

If you're putting up with things you know aren't right you're changing who you are just to keep the wrong person in your life.

Most women know when they're holding onto Mr. Wrong, but they think they can fix him up, and change him into Mr. Right.

In order to hold onto Mr. Wrong, you have to do the following.

1. You have to lower your self-respect.
2. You have to love yourself less than you should.
3. You have to look dumb, stupid or foolish.
4. You have to put up with disrespect.
5. You have to put up with things that you know aren't right.
6. You have to settle for a man that will never give you 100% of himself.
7. You have to let a man walk all over you or take advantage of you.
8. You have to be with a man that doesn't care about your happiness.
9. You have to be with a man that always puts himself before you.
10. You have to be with a man that doesn't love you the way you should be loved.
11. You have to be with a man that thinks it's OKAY to treat you like crap.
12. You have to be with a man that hurts you over and over again because your feelings don't matter to him.
13. You have to be with a man that will never love you the way that you love him.
14. You have to be with a man that doesn't take care of your emotional needs.

The above list consists of things that a woman shouldn't have to do or put up with in a relationship or in life. If a woman is putting up with the above things she is settling for less, she doesn't know her worth, and she is holding onto Mr. Wrong. Even though that list is horrible, and most women don't want to admit that they've held onto a Mr. Wrong. The truth is that most women have been with a Mr. Wrong, and some are still holding onto a Mr. Wrong. If that list describes your relationship or it describes the type of man you're holding onto you're holding onto Mr. Wrong. If he were Mr. Right he would be the total opposite of all those things. Realize that Mr. Wrong won't make you happy. He might make you happy sometimes, but the more you hold onto him the more you'll realize that he cares about his own happiness more than your happiness. Also, you'll realize that he isn't giving you what you need, but you're giving him everything you've got, and more.

BLINDED BY LOVE?

They say love is blind but I say 'love sees everything, but it ignores what it sees.' Basically, no matter how much a woman loves Mr. Wrong she knows he isn't treating her right or loving her the way that he should. If his love were so great that it blinded her she wouldn't be able to see his bad behavior or other things he does wrong. The fact that she does see it, and it saddens her or breaks her heart, shows that it isn't blinding her at all. A woman sees Mr. Wrong's bad side, but she ignores it or overlooks it because she doesn't want to leave him, and she thinks she can fix their relationship. She puts up with his disrespect and other things she knows she shouldn't put up with hoping that he'll change and that things will go back to how it used to be. Hope is a good thing, but sometimes you have to realize that what you're hoping for is unrealistic and move on.

THE MAGICAL GIRL

Every time there's a movie about a jerk, player or guy who just wants sex there's a girl in the movie that gets him to change into this sweetheart of a guy. Something about this girl makes him give up his old ways and change into this great new guy. Well, that makes a plot for a good movie, but in reality that usually isn't what happens. However, a lot of women these days have taken the bait, hook line and sinker. They actually believe that they can change a jerk into a really nice guy. So, they try to become the magical girl that enters into his life and changes his life forever. They pull every trick they can and try to get this man to magically change his ways for them. However, when a woman's 'magic' get him to change tricks' don't work she begins to think less of herself. Since she can't get him to change she thinks something is wrong with her, and that she isn't good enough to make him change. Even though what she's doing isn't changing him she continues to try because she wants to be the magical girl that gets him to change. Are you trying to be Mr. Wrong's game changer? The girl that gets him to change into a nice guy? Have movies like this influenced you? These player movies are just an adult version of the princess and the frog. The princess is the magical girl that kisses a frog and changes him into prince charming. Women grow up watching these movies, and they spend a great part of their life trying to be the magical girl that changes the frog into a prince or should I say jerk into a nice guy or should I say friend with benefits into a real boyfriend. The problem is that the jerk isn't changing because he met a magical girl, he's changing because he wants to change. That's right. There comes a point in most men's life where they decide that they are ready to settle down, but until they reach that point they run from relationships. Until a man is ready to settle down nothing you do or say will get him to settle down. Some men refuse to settle down until they are able to provide for a woman, and kids if they want them. Basically, if a man isn't offering you the type of relationship that you want just move on. Also, if he isn't the type of guy you're looking for just move on. Stop trying to change jerks into nice guys. They have to change themselves, and unfortunately, some jerks will never change. After a man decides to change he will come across a woman that he feels that he can settle down with. This girl isn't magical it's just that she came into his life at a point that he was ready to settle down, and she fit his description of the 'one'. I will discuss this in more detail later on. If a man settles down before he is ready to settle down or change his single ways the woman he settles down with won't be too happy with his cheating, disrespectful ways. Therefore, you should never force or pressure a man into settling when he isn't ready.

HE CHANGED?

Some people are good at hiding who they really are. When you first meet them they hide who they really are, and they only show you their good side. Then months or even years later you see the other side of them. Not because they've changed, but because you've finally caught them. There are some women who married a man and later found out that he had been cheating the whole time. He didn't change into a cheater, she just finally caught him. A woman gets beat up by her boyfriend of 1 year during an argument. Did he become an abuser overnight or was that side of him lurking inside of him? Chances are he already had a temper, but he was just controlling it until he couldn't control it anymore and lashed out at her. Sometimes you have to realize that the person you're with hasn't changed they're just not hiding who they are anymore. Most people like this don't show you their true colors until they have you wrapped around your fingers. They know you won't leave them so they think it's safe to show you their true colors. Or they finally slip, and you find out their true colors on your own. Either way, you need to realize that what they're showing you is the real them, and it's who they always were. Never think that you did something to cause them to treat you wrong or that you made them change into such a horrible person. Some women think that if he used to treat them right, then they must have done something to make him treat them wrong. Or that if he used to love them that they must have done something to make him not love them anymore. This type of thinking is wrong because you're blaming yourself for his actions. His actions are his choice, not your choice. Never blame yourself for someone else's actions or choices. Also, if some women really look at their past they'll see the red flags Mr. Wrong gave them, and they'll also admit that they ignored those red flags. They ignored those red flags because they didn't want to mess up what they thought was a good thing. From now on don't ignore those red flags. When you first meet Mr. Wrong you'll enjoy his company, but you'll also see dozens of red flags. Don't ignore them just to keep him in your life.

EXCUSES WON'T CHANGE THE TRUTH

When some women can't handle the truth they make up excuses for what's happening to them. Mr. Wrong could be showing them dozens of signs that he isn't interested in them, but they will make up an excuse for why he's acting that way. They want to believe that Mr. Wrong loves them even though it's obvious that he doesn't. He's ignoring them, not making time for them, and he's treating them wrong but they think he's in love with them? They think he's too scared to be with them or that he's afraid to tell them how he feels about them or that he loves them but he doesn't know it yet or that he's hiding his true feelings for them. So, they chase after him and try to make him realize that he's in love with them. *"Hey guy you're completely and madly in love with me, but you just don't know it yet, but I'm going to make you realize that you are.* A guy knows if he's in love with you or not and if he's in love with you, you'll know it. If he's in love with you, he's not going to ignore you or reject you. If you actually think someone that ignores you, doesn't make time for you, avoids you, and doesn't want anything to do with you loves you you're avoiding the truth. If you actually think a guy that doesn't want to commit to you or be with you loves you, you're avoiding the truth. Stop telling yourself that a man that mistreats, disrespects or uses you loves you. You're lying to yourself because you can't handle the truth. If he loved you he would be chasing after you and begging you to be in his life. If he loved you he would be happy to talk to you and he wouldn't be ignoring you. If he loved you he'd be happy to spend time with you, and he wouldn't be avoiding you. If he loved you he would make an effort to be in your life. He'd fight to be in your life. If he isn't fighting for you then he isn't into you. Stop lying to yourself just to make yourself feel better. In order to move on you have to face the truth.

Answer the two questions below truthfully. Be honest, and don't lie to yourself:

1. Is he acting like he's in love with you or like he's NOT in love with you?
2. Is he acting like he's into you or like he's NOT into you?

If NOT you have to face the truth, and stop lying to yourself. The truth hurts, but the sooner you accept it the sooner you can deal with it and move on.

HOLDING ONTO MR. WRONG

Women know when they're holding onto Mr. Wrong, but something about him makes them feel as if they need him in their life. They hold onto him because they think they can be the woman that changes him or fixes him into the type of man that they're looking for. Even though he's offering them less than what they're looking for, they're hoping that he'll give them more one day. The little bit of happiness that he gives them makes them put up with the misery. They aren't holding onto the Mr. Wrong that everyone else sees, they're holding onto a man that has shown them that he has the potential to be a better man than he is. The Mr. Wrong they're holding onto has shown them a side of him that he hasn't shown her family or her friends. So, her family and friends are confused as to why she's holding onto a loser. When her family and friends see him they see a man that isn't good for her, and a man that isn't treating her right. However, when she sees him she sees a man that's loving, caring, fun, and makes her happy. She holds onto him because she thinks he's a broken guy that needs her help, and her love. Women that hold onto Mr. Wrong are usually fixers. They're always trying to fix a broken man or fix a relationship that they should leave. They hold onto Mr. Wrong because they want to fix him and make him happy. They think that if they fix him he'll be the guy they fell in love with, and he'll stop treating them wrong. When he acts like the beast they still see the prince in him. To them, he's a beast that can be tamed with the right amount of love or affection. A beast they can change into the prince that they are looking for. Even if he treats them wrong they still think it's their job to make him happy. Even if he isn't showing them love, they'll still give him all of their love. Even though he treats them wrong most of the time he has also shown them that he isn't 100% bad. He can treat them wrong 90% of the time, and right 10% of the time and they'll stick around just to get that 10%. Why? It's because they think he'll eventually give them 100%. These women don't hold onto him thinking that they'll always be treated wrong. They hold onto him because they believe that things will change and that he will treat them right one day. They believe that he'll change his behavior, step up to the plate, and be the man that they think he can be. However, he will never be the man they want him to be because that's not who he is and that's not who he wants to be. In order to let go of Mr. Wrong, you have to realize that you're holding onto a dream instead of reality. The dream is who you want him to be, and reality is who he really is. The dream is how you want him to treat you, and reality is how he's really treating you.

Realize that the real him is the man that you dislike. It's the side of him that he has shown you from time to time. You've seen his true colors, but you try to look past them or ignore them. You've seen his true colors but you make excuses for his behavior, and how he treats you. In order to let go of him you have to face the truth, and look at what you're really holding onto. What kind of man are you holding onto? Let's talk about the real him. You know the side of him that you pretend doesn't exist?

1. The real him is the man that keeps cheating on you over and over again with different women.
2. The real him is the man that blacks your eyes when he gets mad at you, and then apologizes for it.
3. The real him is the man that refuses to commit to you or be with you, but still wants to sleep with you.
4. The real him is the man that only calls you when he wants something from you.
5. The real him is the man that doesn't care about you, and you know he doesn't care about you because he's never there for you.
6. The real him is the man that isn't showing you the love you need, deserve or want.
7. The real him is the man that thinks it's okay to treat you like your nothing like you're worthless
8. The real him is the man that uses you for sex, and you know he's using you for sex because after you have sex with him you feel used.

However, you ignore the real side of him, and act like that side of him doesn't exist. Every day you live a lie and pretend like he's this great guy when he's far from it. Sure he has a sweet side that pops up every now and then, but the real him is the side of him that you hate. The side of him that you're trying to change, and the side of him that hurts you or breaks your heart. Once you see Mr. Wrongs true colors don't sugar coat it or try to paint a pretty picture with it. His true colors are who he really is, and if you don't like his true colors move on. Don't put up with his bad side just to get those sweet crumbs that he throws at you from time to time. Are you holding onto Mr. Wrongs good side or his bad side? Are you ignoring the bad side, and pretending like it doesn't exist? Is his bad side making you miserable? Is his bad side showing you love or is it hurting you? In order to let go of Mr. Wrong, you have to face the cold truth. Stop holding onto who you want him to be or who you think he can be, and look at who he really is. What does he do to you that hurts you or makes you cry? You've separated him into two people. One is the person that you think loves you, and the other is the person that you know doesn't love you. So, you focus on the side of him that shows you love, and you ignore the side that doesn't. Stop dividing him up into 2 people. The side you love and the side you hate are both him. You have to accept both sides of him or move on. If you're trying to get rid of the bad side and keep the good side you're trying to change him. Some women waste months or years trying to change Mr. Wrong into the man of their dreams. When some women think about leaving Mr. Wrong he shows them his good side, and they stay with him. Once a woman has seen Mr. Wrongs good side she'll put up with his bad side for months or years just to enjoy his good side. Basically, the good side of him is her dream guy, and she's hoping that he will become that guy at all times not just sometimes.

Mr. Wrong will confuse you

Mr. Wrong confuses a woman, and she tries to figure him out. She will spend months or years trying to figure out why he does the things he does. Or she will try to figure out if he loves her or not.

She will ask questions like:

1. Why does a man that says he loves her act like he hates her?
2. Why does he act like she's his everything one day, and then the next day treat her like she doesn't mean anything to him?

3. Why does he utter the words "I love you" and then cheats on her, disrespects her, uses her, beats her or walks all over her?
4. Why does Mr. Wrong keep you around for months or years without committing to you or taking things to the next level?
5. Why does Mr. Wrong act like he's in love with you, but refuses to be with you or commit to you?

A woman holding onto Mr. Wrong will ask herself these questions, and she'll want these answers from her Mr. Wrong. So, she'll ask him questions like "Why did you cheat on me?" or "How could you do that to me?" A woman holding onto a man that refuses to commit to her might be too afraid to ask anything. So, she just stands by Mr. Wrongs side and hopes that he'll commit to her one day. When you ask Mr. Wrong questions chances are he'll just give you excuses or lies instead of the truth. Some women know he's lying, but since they can't handle the truth they ignore their instincts and stay with him. In the future, instead of asking Mr. Wrong questions ask yourself questions.

Questions like

1. Why are you holding onto a man that keeps cheating on you?
2. Why are you giving everything you've got to a man that refuses to commit to you?
3. Why are you letting him hurt you over and over again?
4. Why are you having sex with a man that only wants sex from you?

Stop asking Mr. Wrong questions and start asking yourself **"Why you're settling for less and why are you putting up with things you know aren't right?"** You know he's treating you wrong, and something inside of you is telling you that you should move on, but you refuse to listen to it. The reason you refuse to listen to it is because you think you can fix everything, and change him from Mr. Wrong into Mr. Right. You think all your love and nurturing will change him into the man of your dreams. You think he'll wake up one day and realize what he has, and start appreciating you. You think he'll wake up one day, get on one knee, and ask you to marry him or commit to you. So, you hold onto him and you try your best to make that happen. You change who you are, you fix yourself up, you try to make him happy, and you give him your all. Yet he still doesn't change into the guy of your dreams. Do you know why? It's because he's Mr. Wrong, and he'll always be Mr. Wrong. If he were Mr. Right he would be treating you right. Realize that the wrong person makes you beg for love, affection, and a commitment. The right person gives you those things because they love you. Realize that every love story doesn't have a happy ending. The fairy tales you grew up watching always had a happy ending. The prince would show up to rescue the princess, and they would live happily ever after. However, Mr. Wrong hasn't shown up to rescue you he has shown up to take advantage of you, disrespect you, cheat on you, use you, beat you or walk all over you, and the sad thing is you're letting him get away with it. You're putting up with things you know you shouldn't be putting up with. You're letting a man think it's okay to disrespect you, cheat on you, beat you, use you for sex or walk all over you. What he's doing to you shouldn't be okay with you. What he's doing shouldn't be tolerated or put up with. The problem is that you put him way before you. His happiness matters to you more than your own. Also, you love him more than you love yourself. You look out for him, but you don't look out for yourself. If you were looking out for yourself, you'd follow your instincts and leave Mr. Wrong. When you stay you're not looking out for yourself you're keeping yourself in harm's way. If you had your own back, you'd watch it not let a man stab you in it over and over again. Realize that you have to choose between taking care of yourself, and taking care of Mr. Wrong. If he isn't treating you right you have to do what's best for you and leave. Also, if Mr. Wrong was taking care of you like he should you wouldn't feel as if he didn't love you or care about you. Mr. Wrong will make you feel like you're not good enough for him. If you stay with him you'll question your worth, and you'll begin to think you're not worth that much. When a man is acting like you're not good enough that's a sign that he's Mr. Wrong. Mr. Right will treat you like a Queen and you'll know he loves you because his actions will prove that he does.

CARING FOR MR. WRONG

Most women will care about a man before he is even her man. As soon as some women meet a guy they're interested in they begin to care about his well-being, and they begin to think of ways that they can improve his life. There's nothing wrong with caring about a man, but caring for the wrong man leads to heartbreak. Since most women are naturally very caring people they take it upon themselves to care for everyone in their life. If they feel like they can help someone in their life they will help them. However, women need to realize that they shouldn't do too much for someone that isn't committed to them yet. When some women think they can fix the guy they've just met, the empathetic, caring part of them wants to help him. In fact, that part of them will begin to list ways that they can help him, and he will become their project. The guy they barely know has no idea that they've already planned what they will do with him, and what they've already planned to do for him. He was just thinking about the first date, and they're already thinking about things they want to do with him months from now. The caring part of you can't be turned on and off at will, but there are a few things you can do to prevent yourself from being used too much. Women that care too much get used a lot because they tend to give all they've got to the wrong people. Whenever they care about someone they break their back to make that person happy. So, when they meet a guy they care about they break their back to make him happy even though he's not committed to them or in love with them yet. What these women can do is take things slow. When you first meet a guy don't go out of your way to make him happy. He's not your man, boyfriend or husband so you shouldn't be treating him like he is. Secondly, if you just met him why are you thinking of a list of things you can do to fix him up or help him out? If you just met him, and you're already thinking of ways you can change him he's Mr. Wrong. If you just met him, and you're already thinking of ways that you can help him out you're the type of woman that gets used a lot because you're always breaking your back for men that haven't committed to you yet. Stop investing so much of yourself into men that you don't know, and men that aren't committed to you. The only man that you should be breaking your back for is a man that is breaking his back for you. The next time you meet a man, take things slow and don't try to win him over with acts of kindness. Also, don't spoil him or break your back for him until he's committed to you. Giving everything you've got to a man that doesn't plan on being with you is a waste of time. When you first meet a guy you don't know what his intentions are. He could just be looking for sex, and here you go treating him like he's your boyfriend. He could have just been looking for sex, but you started cleaning for him, cooking for him and spoiling him, and now you're just his 'friend with benefits'. Save all that wife stuff for your future husband. Basically, it's okay to care about the guy you've just met, but don't invest everything you've got into him, and don't break your back for him either. Find out what the new guy wants from you before you act like you're his wife.

Your instincts and common sense will tell you the truth.

Most women have very good intuition or instincts. They know when something isn't right. Mr. Wrongs words aren't adding up, his actions are disrespectful, his behavior is changing and he doesn't treat her how he used to. Things just don't seem right, and you feel as if he isn't right for you. He doesn't take care of your emotional needs, and there's a part of you that he never seems to connect with. Usually, a woman can tell when her boyfriend or husband is cheating on her because things seem a bit off, and he acts a little distant. It's a feeling that you can't shake, and sure enough, you're eventually faced with the truth. Now, what you do with that truth depends on how you value yourself. When a man is using you for sex your instincts, and common sense will tell you that it's just sex to him. You'll feel used because your instincts and common sense will tell you that's all he seems to want from you. Women have the used feeling, but they ignore what their body is telling them because they think Mr. Wrong will want more than sex one day. They think he'll get to know more about them, and fall in love with them. Some women know when a man isn't interested in them, but they ignore their gut instinct and chase after him anyway. From now on follow your instincts and common sense. When Mr. Wrong is playing you, using you or cheating on you, your instincts will tell you that something isn't right.

What's his definition of love?

One thing that some Mr. Wrongs have in common is their definition of the word 'love'. They confuse caring about a woman more than they care about other women with love. Think about your guy friends. Even though you're not in love with them romantically you still love them and care about their well-being. Well, some Mr. Wrongs feel that way about you. They're not in love with you, but they still care about you, and they love you as a friend. So, when some men say they love you they actually believe that they do. However, their actions, and how they treat you proves that they're not in love with you. Their actions also prove that they're not committed to you or the relationship. When you first meet a guy ask questions like "What's your definition of love?" Do you think you can cheat on someone, and still be in love with them?" Have you ever cheated on someone you loved?" "What do you consider cheating?" Some men will actually tell you that they've cheated on someone they loved but regretted it. However, you have to realize that their answer reveals that they're capable of being unfaithful to someone that they claim to love. If he doesn't agree with you on 'what's considered cheating, and 'what you shouldn't do in a committed relationship' move on. If you get involved with someone that doesn't have the same morals or beliefs that you have it won't work out because they will constantly do things that you don't agree with. Yet they will think it's perfectly normal or acceptable. It's better to find out his morals or beliefs when you first meet him than it is to find out months or years later. A few getting to know you questions could save you from heartbreak.

ARE YOU IN LOVE WITH MR. WRONG?

Some women think they're in love with Mr. Wrong, but the truth is they're holding onto him to fix issues they have within themselves. Below are 6 things women confuse with love.

It's lust not love

This Mr. Wrong knows he's good in bed, and he knows how to satisfy you sexually. Sex with him is always good, and the sexual chemistry you have with him is phenomenal. When you sleep together it feels as if you two belong together because your bodies connect so well, and the sex is probably the best you've ever had. The way he kisses you, caresses you, and makes love to you makes you feel good. However, outside of the bedroom you two aren't connected. Outside of the bedroom, it doesn't seem that he loves you or like he's into you. Inside of the bedroom, it seems like he's in love with you, and he's making love to you. However, you should never judge a guy by how he treats you in the bedroom because whether some men are in love with you or not they'll still have sex with you. Judge a man by how he treats you outside of the bedroom because that's when he's thinking with the head on his shoulders and not the head in his pants. Some women think they're in love with Mr. Good Sex however they're just addicted to his sex. If you ask them what they love about this guy 'sex' will be the first thing that pops into their head followed by other physical things. If you ask them what they like about the guy besides his sex they won't have much to say. What's the first thing that pops into your head about the guy you're dating? If it's sex you're not in love with him you're in lust with him. Chances are this guy doesn't do anything for you emotionally or mentally, and you might not even like his personality or lifestyle. Plus, he might not even be your type. Is he the type of guy that you want to marry, and have a family with? If he asked you to marry him right now what would your answer be? If 'no' or 'not sure' or you have to 'think about it' you're not in love with him, you just like having sex with him. His sex is so good that it keeps you coming back for more. His sex is so good that it has fooled you into thinking that you love a man that isn't even your type. If sex is the only thing you like about him let him go. Find a guy that has more to offer you than just sex. Good sex can cure loneliness temporarily, but real love can cure it permanently. Also, Mr. Good Sex uses sex to fix problems that you have with him. Anytime there's an argument or problem he tries to fix it with sex. He knows that getting you into bed will make you forgive him. However, realize that good sex doesn't fix relationship problems it just covers it up temporarily. Until you deal with the problem it will continue to resurface.

It's memories not love

When you met this Mr. Wrong everything was perfect to you. You got along with him well, and you did a lot of fun things together. He used to be so sweet and romantic. He said the right things and did the right things. For once you were happy, and you had a guy that you were comfortable with. You could actually see yourself spending the rest of your life with him. Everything was going great. Well, at least you thought it was. Until he cheated on you or did something else to you that broke your heart. The day he broke your heart it hurt, and you saw a different side of him. A side of him you'd never seen before. It's like you knew him, but you didn't know him. He did something to you that you thought he'd never do. He wasn't treating you the same as he did before. All his "I love yous' kept replaying in your head, and you wondered if ever meant it. You didn't want to leave him, but how could you stay when he did something that you didn't approve of? If you stayed you would become a woman that allowed a man to disrespect her. You didn't want to lower your worth or settle for less, but you also didn't want to leave him. How could you leave someone that made you so happy? Well, at least he used to before he disrespected you or hurt you. If you left you would be protecting yourself, loving yourself, and getting rid of a man that didn't love you like he claimed. However, after he apologized, and you thought it over you swallowed your pride and stayed even though a part of you told you that you should leave. You stayed because you thought you could fix things, and go back to how it used to be. Now, you're holding onto a man you can't trust. Sure he apologized, but you still can't trust him. Trust is an important part of a relationship, and that's one thing you don't have with him. If you're holding onto this Mr. Wrong you're holding onto what used to be, you're holding onto the memories, and you're holding onto a man that you can't trust. Do you want to marry a man that you can't trust? Do you want to spend the rest of your life with a man that you can't trust? When he hurt you that day he showed you his true colors, but you ignored it and kept holding onto him. If he asked you to marry him right now what would you say? If 'no' or 'not sure' you're not in love with him you're just holding onto memories, and what used to be.

Loneliness, good sex, and good memories can make you go back to Mr. Wrong. Always remember the real reasons you're not with him, and stay strong.

It's loneliness not love

This Mr. Wrong is fun to be around. You like hanging out with him, and you enjoy his company. Whenever you're lonely or bored you can call him up, and have someone to spend time with. The only reason you're keeping him around is because you don't have anyone else to spend time with. If you met someone else you were interested in you wouldn't need or want this guy anymore. Ask yourself this question "If I met a sweet guy today to spend time with, and do fun things with would I still be interested in the guy I'm holding onto now?" Do you only think about this guy when you're bored, lonely or want company? Is he your type? Are you holding onto him because you're comfortable with him, and he's your only choice? Chances are if you had more choices, better choices you'd forget about this guy. If he asked you to marry him right now what would your answer be? If 'no' you're not interested in him you're just lonely, and you're using him to pass time. Once you find someone else to cure your loneliness you'll forget all about this Mr. Wrong.

It's validation, not love.

You will ask yourself "Why doesn't he love me? Or "What's wrong with me?" Or "Why doesn't he want to be with me?"

This Mr. Wrong makes you feel like you're not good enough for him. Since he doesn't want to be with you, you think that something is wrong with you. You hate feeling like something is wrong with you, and you hate feeling like you're not good enough for him. So, you're constantly thinking of ways that you can get him to be with you, and you're constantly trying to figure out why he doesn't want to be with you. You think he doesn't want to commit to you because you're not pretty enough or good enough for him. So, you start doing whatever you can to make him want to be with you. You might change your appearance, you might show him a lot of love, you might go out of your way to please him, and you might change who you are just to get him to like you. All day long you're thinking of ways that you can get him to love you or be with you. You think you're in love with him, but the truth is you're seeking validation. You want him to tell you that you're good enough. When a guy doesn't think you're good enough for him you question your worth. You need a guy's approval just to feel good about yourself. This guy is always on your mind because you're always thinking of ways that you can make him love you. When you think about this guy do you think about how much you love him or do you think about how he doesn't love you? If you think about how he doesn't love you more than you think about how much you're in love with him you're seeking validation. If you never think about how much you love him you're definitely not in love with him, and you're a chaser. Do you constantly think of ways that you can get him to commit to you or fall in love with you? Are you constantly trying to figure out why he doesn't want to commit to you? Do you hate feeling like you're not good enough? Do you think that something is wrong with you just because he doesn't want to be with you? Are you trying to prove your worth to him? Are you doing everything you can to make him happy just so he'll fall in love with you? If you answered 'yes' to the above questions you chase men just to feel good about yourself. You need a man's approval just to feel good about yourself, and you let men tell you how much you're worth. When a man doesn't want to be with you, you think something is wrong with you, but the truth is he's just wrong for you. If the guy you're chasing asked you to marry him right now what would your answer be? If 'no' you're not in love with him you're just chasing him because you can't handle rejection. When a guy rejects you, you chase after him and try to make him love you. However, you should just move on. In my book '25 Steps to Letting Go of Someone You Love' I go over this in more detail.

It's a challenge not love

This Mr. Wrong confuses you. He claims to love you, but he constantly disrespects you. He has two sides to him. One side you love, and one side you hate. The side you love or think you love gives you goosebumps, and makes you happy. It's the side that won your heart and still has your heart. The side you hate makes you miserable. It's the side that makes you want to leave him, and it's the side you wish you could change about him. The only reason you're holding onto him is because you love his good side, and you think you can change his bad side. He has become a challenge to you. If you can't fix him you think something is wrong with you. If you can fix him, it means that you're good enough and that you're doing something right. You base your worth as a woman on being able to keep your man happy and keep your man from cheating on you. If he isn't happy or he's cheating on you, you blame yourself and think that you must be doing something wrong. You see him as an extension of you. When he misbehaves you always find a way to blame his behavior on you. He has become your project, and you're trying to change him from Mr. Wrong into Mr. Right. You might make demands or give ultimatums to try to force him to change. You might threaten to leave him or you might try to keep your eyes on him more. You're constantly trying to figure out why he keeps treating you wrong, and you're constantly trying to fix what you think might be wrong. You think that if you can just fix his issues or problems that he'll be the perfect guy for you. When one thing doesn't work or stop him from hurting you, you try to think of something else. He challenges you because you think it's your job to make him love you or treat you right. Some women spend months or years trying to make a guy treat them right. Realize that you can't make a man treat you right. If he isn't treating you right he's telling you where you stand with him. How a man treats you is how he feels about you. You can't make a man do something he doesn't want to do, if he isn't doing it on his own he doesn't want to do it. Realize that his bad side is the real him. The man that says he loves you is disrespecting you, walking all over you, abusing you or cheating on you. Stop blaming yourself for his actions. He knows right from wrong he just chooses to treat you wrong. Just because you can't change him it doesn't mean that you're not a real woman or that you're not good enough. As soon as you start thinking of ways that you can fix a man, make him treat you right or make him be with you, you need to realize that you're holding onto a Mr. Wrong. Do you constantly think of ways that you can get him to stop cheating on you? Are you constantly thinking of ways that you can make him treat you right or change him? Do you think his bad behavior is your fault? Do you think something is wrong with you, and that if you fix it he'll treat you better? Do you think he'll love you if you changed who you are or fixed yourself up? Do you think it's your fault that he treats you wrong? Do you think the woman he cheats on you with have something that you don't have, and you're trying to figure out what it is? Do you think something is wrong with you, and you're trying to figure out what it is so he'll love you? If you answered 'yes' to any of the above questions you see him as a challenge. Fixing him up, and making him love you or treat you right makes you feel like a real or good woman. You base your worth on how men treat you. If men treat you well you think you're a Queen or a good woman. If they treat you wrong you think something is wrong with you, and that you're worthless or not good enough. When he behaves you think it's because you're making him happy, but when he misbehaves you think it's because you're making him unhappy. Is he the type of guy that you want to marry? Do you want to put up with what he does for the rest of your life? Is this how you want to be treated? If he asked you to marry him right now what would your answer be? If your answer would be 'no' or 'not sure' you're not in love with him you're just holding onto his good side. Deep down inside you know you deserve better, and you know he's Mr. Wrong. Even though he makes you happy sometimes it's not worth all the tears and disrespect. All you want is for a man to love you just like you love him. You don't want a man that makes you feel worthless; you want a man that makes you feel like a queen. You don't want a man that is chasing other women and sleeping around on you. You want a man that wants to be with you, and only you. You don't want a man that tells you he loves you one day and then stabs you in the back the next day. You want to settle down with a man that is committed to you and the relationship, not a man that acts like he's single. A woman that knows her worth is ashamed to claim a man that is disrespecting her and making her look stupid or foolish. Only claim a man that is worthy to be claimed, a man that lets the world know that you're the girl that has his heart. Not with words, but with his actions, and his willingness to commit to you and the relationship.

Realize that letting go of a bad relationship doesn't mean that you've failed or that you weren't good enough to make it work; it means that it wasn't meant to be.

It's the chase not love

This Mr. Wrong doesn't want to be with you, and deep down inside you don't want to be with him either. However, you're a woman that is used to getting what you want, and when a man doesn't want to be with you, you see it as a challenge. When a man isn't into you, you chase after him, try to seduce him, and try to make him love you. However, once you catch him or he shows interest in you, you lose interest in him. Men that adore you or want you aren't your type, and they bore you. Men that ignore you are interesting to you, and you're constantly thinking of ways that you can make them want you. Men that reject you are always on your mind, and you're constantly thinking of ways that you can get them to chase after you. Unlike the women who chase for validation this woman chases for fun, and as a game. This woman sees herself as someone that men should want, and when a man doesn't want her she tries to figure out why her usual charm isn't working with this guy. It becomes a game to her, a puzzle that she has to piece together. If she wins him over she wins the game or solves the puzzle. If she doesn't win him over she begins to think that her sex appeal or charm isn't as good as she thinks it is. If she never wins him over her self-esteem or self- worth will begin to lower, and then she might start chasing him for validation. However, once she wins him over whether it was for the chase or validation she loses interest in him. Some chasers will start arguments or unnecessary drama with a guy they've caught just to get him to leave. Once he leaves they will start chasing him again and try to win him back. Again the chaser needs to be chasing a guy in order for her to be interested in him. Even if she has to push him away on purpose she will do it just so she can chase him again. Men who chase her aren't interesting to her, and men she has already caught are not interesting to her. 50 men could be chasing her, but she would only be interested in the guy that isn't chasing her because she sees him as different and more of a challenge. Is the guy you're chasing your type? Are you only interested in men that you have to chase after? Which type of men do you think about the most? Men, that are interested in you or men that act like they're not interested in you? Are you constantly thinking of ways that you can seduce men and make them fall for you? Are you used to getting your way with men, and when a man doesn't show interest in you it bothers you and makes you question your worth? Do men that chase after you or give you too much attention bore you? When a guy you're chasing shows interest in you do you feel like you've just won a game or like you've gotten him to fall for your charm, game or spell? Once you catch a guy you're chasing do you think he's just like the rest of the guys or do you still think of him as different? If your opinion of him changes right after you catch him, and you begin to think he's like the rest you're definitely a chaser because you only think a guy is different or special when you can't have him. Once you catch him his specialness wears off, and you don't see him as different from other men anymore. If you caught the guy you're chasing, and he asked you to marry him right now what would your answer be? If your answer would be 'no' you're a chaser, and you're not in love with him you just like playing cat, and mouse. Of course, you would be the cat because you have more fun being the cat.

The opposite of a chaser is a woman that likes to be chased.

Some women are the total opposite because they like being the mouse. They like when men chase after them, but they get a kick out of not being caught. They want men to chase them or give them attention, but they have no intention of letting those men catch them. Basically, they're a teaser, not a pleaser. If you like men to chase you even though you're not interested in them you hold onto Mr. Wrongs because you like the attention they give you. Chances are you might be lonely, and you'll take whatever attention you can get or you just like when men compliment you or want you. You like seducing men and making them chase after you. Be careful if you're this type of woman because it's not nice to lead people on. Most women like this are afraid of intimacy. They like getting close to men but not close enough to get hurt. Or they need attention from men to feel good about themselves or they like to play games with men or toy with them. If you're not careful this type of behavior can lead to you becoming a player.

It's pain not love

This Mr. Wrong treats you wrong, and you know he's treating you wrong, but you're used to it. How he's treating you has become a pattern in your life. You've dealt with men like him most of your life, and you're used to being treated wrong. The pain you feel feels like love to you because that's all you know about love. You've never had someone love you the way you should be loved. You've never had a guy show you, real love. You've only been used, disrespected, abused, cheated on and mistreated by men. You know what the real definition of love is, but you still accept disrespect and call it love. You actually think a man that uses you for sex and cheats on you over and over again loves you. You actually think a man that beats you until you're black and blue loves you or cares about you. You actually think a man that refuses to commit to you or claim you loves you. You think being treated like crap is love? Why? It's because that's how men have always treated you. You allow men to treat you like that because deep down inside you don't love yourself as much as you say you do. When a man makes you feel hurt, rejected or in pain you chase after him and try to make him love you. However, you should be running away from him. When you feel the pain you think it's love because that's what love feels like to you. Does thinking about him make your heart break? Does thinking about him make you feel rejected or hurt? Do you feel used after you have sex with him? Do you feel like he's taking advantage of you? Do you feel like he's not in love with you? If thinking about him makes you sad or miserable realize that you're holding onto him because you're addicted to feeling pain. Maybe a guy in your past used you for sex or molested you, and now you're letting other men use you for your body. Maybe other men cheated on you, and now you think it's normal for a man to keep cheating on you. Maybe the men in your past treated you the same way he is and you're used to being treated that way. If what you're feeling is pain it's time to let go of him. Do you want to feel like that for the rest of your life? If he asked you to marry him what would your answer be? If 'no' you're not in love with him you're just holding onto him because you're used to being treated wrong. You're used to the wrong guys treating you wrong, and you're used to the pain. Pain feels like love to you. Realize that there's a big difference between a heart aching because it isn't being loved, and a heart that's beating fast because it's being loved the way it should be. Is your heart aching for the love he isn't giving you or is it beating fast because he's showering you with love? If it's aching move on because what you're feeling isn't love its pain. Don't settle for sprinkles of love, settle for a heavy love that showers you and drenches you. Settle for the type of love you can feel emotionally, mentally, and physically, not just sexually.

It's you trying to earn love the wrong way

Earners are women that try to buy a man's heart. They are always thinking of things they can do for a man that will make him happy. They will give this man everything they've got just to get love or attention from him. They will give him everything he wants from sex to money if they think it will make him happy. An earner knows when a man isn't interested in her, but she thinks that giving him a lot of love, attention and other things will make him fall in love with her. She is constantly changing her looks, life or anything else she thinks he doesn't like about her. When a man rejects her or doesn't want to commit to her she believes that something is wrong with her. She chases after a man that she knows is not interested in her because she thinks that if she says or does the right things he'll fall in love with her. Earners are obsessed with earning love from the wrong men. Men that give them love for free bore them because they are used to men that have wanted something from them or used them for something they have. Since they think all men want something from them they try to figure out what it is. If sex doesn't work they try to find something else that will win him over. The sad part about earners is that they Mr. Wrong doesn't want their heart, but they still offer him other things he wants. If you're always giving all you've got to man that you know aren't interested in you just to get them to like you or love you, you're an earner. Do you want to marry the man you're chasing? If he asked you to marry him right now what would your answer be? If 'no' you're not in love with him. Realize that giving everything you've got to the wrong men will get you used not loved. Stop giving men your body and other things just to get them to like you. Find a man that doesn't have to be bought, a man that loves you for you, and not for what you've got.

It's pleasing him not love

Pleasers are women that only think about the man's happiness, wants or needs. They live their life just to please the man they're into. When they have sex with him it's only to please him. This woman barely thinks about her needs or wants just her man's. When she makes him happy she feels like she is doing her job. Mr. Wrong loves pleasers because they will do everything to make him happy, and he doesn't have to do anything for them. Most pleasers are women that were molested or abused my men in the past, and now they think women are supposed to please men. Which would be true in a loving relationship, but not in a bad relationship. The pleaser pleases men even if she knows they aren't interested in her. She gives men everything she's got just to satisfy their needs and wants. She has sex with men that she knows isn't interested in her because she is used to men that don't love her using her for sex or her body. If this describes you, you're repeating your past with these men. If you know a man doesn't love you then why are you pleasing him and giving him everything you've got. It's because you're used to men like that. You're used to men who don't love you wanting what you've got. You're used to men who don't love you touching you sexually or having sex with you? Are you constantly with men like this? If so, realize that all men aren't after you for just sex. Of course, your future mate will want to sleep with you, but when he sleeps with you, he will want to please you too. Also, when you sleep with a guy that loves you he'll make sure that you know that you're more than just sex to him. He will commit to you, take care of you, and make you happy too. Realize that shouldn't be and you don't have to please Mr. Wrong or take care of his sexual needs or other needs. You can say 'no' to him and walk away from him without giving him anything. Do you want to marry the man you're pleasing? If he asked you to marry him right now what would your answer be? If 'no' you're not in love with him.

Basically, if this guy isn't your type, and he's not the guy you want to marry or spend the rest of your life with you're not in love with him. You're just holding onto him because you're trying to fix issues you have with yourself. Once you know your worth you won't need a man to make you feel like a woman, and you won't need a man to make you feel good about yourself. You'll no longer feel like something is wrong with you just because a man doesn't want you or doesn't treat you right. Once you know your worth when a man isn't treating you right you'll put the blame on him instead of yourself. In chapter 2 we will go over self-worth because in order to let go of Mr. Wrong you must know your worth.

TYPES OF MR WRONGS
Realize that a person that goes in and out of your life only sees you as an option.

Mr. In and out

Mr. In an Out goes in and out of your life. Sometimes he acts interested in you, and sometimes he ignores you. He confuses you because one day you're having long sweet conversations with him, and he seems very interested in you. Then the next day or week he acts distant or acts like he's not into you, and he ignores you or barely talks to you. Then he acts interested in you again, and the cycle repeats. You take him back because you enjoy the attention he gives you. Even though it's not much you feel as if something can still come out of what you have with him. Sometimes Mr. In and out will vanish for weeks or months and then pop back up like nothing happened. He might even blame you for his disappearance. Most guys like this will give you a dumb excuse for why they disappeared. The excuse Mr. In and Out gives you doesn't make sense, and you don't believe it, but you take him back anyway. Usually, when he comes back he says he misses you, and since you miss him too you take him back. However, after you let him back into your life he acts well for a while then starts blowing hot and cold again. Whenever he blows cold you think something you said or did made him pull away from you. So, you beg him to come back or you chase after him and try to make him interested in you again. However, you should realize that this guy only sees you as an option. He comes back to you when he doesn't have another girl in his life to take care of his needs or wants. Something you're giving him, whether it's sex, company or money is what makes him come back. Then when he doesn't need you anymore or he finds someone else to give him what he wants or needs he vanishes again. No matter how he treats you he knows that you'll take him back. All he has to do is say he misses you or just a simple 'hey' and you'll give him what he wants. To let go of Mr. In and Out you have to realize that you're just an option to him. He can call you up whenever he feels like it, and get whatever he wants from you, then he can just vanish. He doesn't respect you, he's using you, and you're letting him get away with it because you think you can make him love you. NEVER take a guy back that ignored you or vanished out of your life without any explanation. Never let a guy go in and out of your life or he'll take advantage of you. Never chase after a guy that blows hot and cold on you because that's a sign that he isn't interested in you. A guy that's interested in you will blow hot and will act interested in you all the time not sometimes. Think about the guys you call 'desperate'. Those guys always make time for you, there always there for you, and they act like they're interested in you all the time not sometimes. Well, when a guy loves you he doesn't care if loving you makes him look desperate, and he doesn't vanish in and out of your life. Also, when a guy blows cold, acts distant, stops calling, and pulls away from you don't chase him. If he wants to leave let him leave. If you chase after him get ready to get played. When a guy pulls away he's telling you that he's not into you, but if you chase after him, and throw yourself at him he'll take whatever you're throwing at him. One of the biggest mistakes women make is chasing a guy that is pulling away from them because they think they can fix whatever made him pull away. If he pulls away it means he's not into you, it doesn't mean that he wants you to chase after him. If he pulls away he's helping you out because he is cutting himself out of your life. However, if you chase him he isn't going to turn down no strings attached sex, free money or whatever else you have to offer him. This Mr. Wrong comes back when he wants something, then leaves again after he gets it. If you don't give him what he wants he will still leave, but he'll come back later to try to get it again. When you're having a conversation with him he will act interested in the conversation, but his real agenda is to meet up only. You can tell he just wants to meet up because that's what the conversation will lead up to. If you don't want to meet up or give him what he wants the conversation will end because that's the only thing he wanted from you. When you're having a conversation with a guy, and the conversation ends after you don't want to meet him or hang out then it's obvious what he wants from you. Or if he only contacts you when he wants to meet up you should know that he's only looking for a hook-up. Basically, once you find a guy that acts interested in you all the time, and not just sometimes you've found Mr. Right. Let go of Mr. In and Out, and stopping being his option. Your worth more than that.

Stop chasing that jerk and give a nice guy a chance.

Mr. Jerk

Mr. Jerk is very disrespectful, confident and arrogant. Everything has to go his way at all times. He's usually a sarcastic guy who likes to be the center of attention. He talks to women like they're beneath him, and he doesn't have any respect for women. He's rude, and he doesn't care if he says things that will hurt your feelings. Mr. Jerk does whatever he wants, whenever he wants, to whomever he wants. The only person he thinks about is himself. If he needs something you have he'll be sweet to you just to get it, and then he'll be mean to you again after he gets it. People will tell you that "he's nice once you get to know him", but what they really mean is that "you'll get used to his jerkies attitude." Mr. Jerk thinks an apology fixes everything. He will do all kinds of things to you, and then apologize to you like an apology is supposed to make it all better. If you're dealing with a guy that has to apologize to you almost every day for something he did to you, you're dealing with a jerk. His apologies are fake, and he only apologizes to get out of trouble. After he apologizes he goes right back to his jerkish ways and hurts you again. Women hold onto him because he cries when he apologizes, and they feel sorry for him. Or he begs them for another chance or does something really sweet or romantic to win them back. Don't fall for his sweet tricks, because it won't take long before he's disrespecting you again. Find a man that apologizes, and proves that he's sorry by not doing it again.

If you feel like he's using you, it's because your instincts are telling you that you are. So listen.

Mr. User.

Knows he's not in love with you, and he doesn't plan on being with you. Also, he knows that you're in love with him and that you'll do anything to be with him. He goes out looking for women with low self-esteem. Women that he knows he can walk all over, and use. Usually, he can tell if you're the type he wants by how desperate you act or by how much you chase after him. Women that hold onto Mr. User are the type of women that are willing to do anything to be in a relationship with him. They break their back and go out of their way for a man that isn't do anything for them. Even though they feel used they still keep giving him what he wants. They thinking that making him happy will make him fall in love with them. Mr. User only comes around when he wants something. He doesn't help women with their problems, and he takes more than he gives. A woman holding onto this Mr. Wrong will soon realize that she's always there for him, but he's never there for her. Chances are he never calls to see how she's doing. He doesn't care if she's sick or if she's going through hard times. He doesn't take her on romantic dates or spend quality time with her. Yet she keeps holding onto him because she's hoping that always being there for him will make him fall in love with her. Stop breaking your back for a man that won't even break a sweat for you. Stop being there for a man that is never there for you. Stop calling a man that never calls you to see how you're doing or to see if you're okay. He only calls you when he wants to come over or needs something because he's using you. Giving a guy that doesn't love you everything you've got won't get you love it will get you used. If you like feeling used stay with him and continue to let him use you. If you're looking for a guy that will call you up, and see how you're doing move on. If you're looking for a guy that will take you on romantic dates, and take care of you when your sick move on. If you're looking for a guy you can talk to about your problems move on. This Mr. Wrong doesn't care about you or want to be with you, he's just using you.

Realize that a man should use his hands to HOLD his woman not to HIT her.

Mr. Beater

Mr. Beater starts off as a charming guy that is overprotective of you. At first, you think he's just looking out for you, and that he's just the jealous type, but then you realize that he's very controlling. Mr. Beater doesn't know how to communicate his problems verbally so he lets his fist do the talking for him. He seems like a decent guy when everything is going well, but as soon as he gets angry or he can't communicate his feelings properly he lashes out at you. This guy comes off as the jealous type at first because he hate's when other men even look at you. After a while, he starts acting like your dad instead of your partner. He'll tell you what to wear, how to fix your makeup, and he'll start telling you what you can and can't do. Then he makes up rules for you to follow, and if you break his rules he gets angry. He doesn't always tell you these rules, but he will implie them or ask you to change your behavior. If you don't answer the phone after one or 2 rings he gets angry. He'll tell you that he doesn't want you to hang around your girlfriends or go anywhere without him. Basically, you will feel as if you have to check in with him about everything and check in with him throughout the day so he won't get angry or accuse you of things like cheating. At first, he might yell at you, throw things or punch the wall; but after a while, he will slap you out of anger. A slap is the first sign of what's to come. After he slaps you, he will apologize but blame you for what he did. Basically, he'll say he's sorry for what he did, but that you made him angry. Since you've never seen that side of him you're in shock because of what just happened. You might leave him right after he hits you or you might stay because you believe it's your fault. Since it was his first time hitting you, and you've never seen that side of him you might blame yourself for what happened. If you accept his fake apology you're officially entering into a life of a battered woman. When he gets really angry again he will do it again and it will get worse and worse. If Mr. Beater loves the bottle, meaning he's an alcoholic he'll hit you a lot more when he's drunk then he'll blame it on you or the Alcohol. Even though Alcohol can make you act out of the ordinary it's still not an excuse for him to hit you. In fact, there's never a good excuse for him to hit you. If you're with this type of Mr. Wrong get out while you can because some women end up dead when they stay with Mr. Beater too long. Usually, when he gets really angry or he wants to stop a woman from leaving him he'll beat her until she's severely injured or he'll kill her. His good side might be sweet and charming, but the monster that comes out when he's angry is the real him. The real him is a controlling, wife beating manipulator who sees you as his property instead of his partner. He doesn't respect you or your opinions. The only feelings he cares about are his own. Realize that you're not supposed to be a man's property you're supposed to be his wife that he respects. Also, Mr. Beater isn't the type of man you should want to be around or have your kids around. Love yourself, and your kids (if you have them) enough to leave. Never choose Mr. Wrong over your kids or you. There are domestic violence shelters all over the world for women who are victims of domestic violence. If a man hits you call the police, press charges, and move into a domestic violence shelter if you have to. Just get as far away from him as you can, and put a restraining order on him. Once you get the restraining order on him make sure your employer and everyone else in your circle knows that he has to stay away from you. Once you do this you'll have more people looking out for you, and making sure that he stays away from you. If you need the rest of your things have a police officer meet you at his or your place to get it. Never meet up with Mr. Beater by yourself; always have a Cop with you. Mr. Beater will try all kinds of things to get you back, but don't go back. He's just saying sweet things to sucker you back into his life, and regain control over you. If he asks you to meet up with him don't do it. He'll make promises to you, he'll say he has changed, and he'll promise not to do it again. However, you should realize that his apologies are fake, and there just words to him. Always remember the other apologies and promises he gave you that he never meant or kept. If he violates his restraining order report him immediately. A guy that doesn't take a restraining order seriously is a dangerous guy. Keep track of every email, text or call you get from him for evidence. If you feel as if your life is in danger; call the police, and relocate immediately. Move, change numbers, and make sure this guy doesn't know where you're at. Once you find a guy that lets you help make the relationship decisions, let's you have your own opinions, and loves you too much to hit you you've find Mr. Right. Let go of Mr. Beater and stop being his punching bag. Your worth more than that.

A real man compliments you, a weak man insults you and makes you feel as if you're not good enough for him.

Mr. Verbal Abuser

Considers himself outspoken, a comedian or a jokester, but he is far from it. Mr. Verbal Abuser starts off picking at little things about you, things that aren't that big of a deal. However, after you've known him a little longer he begins to insult your looks, your intelligence and other things about you. He might call you fat, ugly, stupid or other names then say you can't take a joke or he's only kidding. However, you know he isn't kidding because he said it in a serious tone. Plus, whether he was kidding or not he shouldn't be saying those things to you. He acts like his insults aren't that big of a deal, and that you're just overreacting. Staying with this type of guy will lower your self-esteem. You will begin to hate the way you look, and you will think you're not good enough for him. You might even begin to believe the things he says about you or try to change who you are for him. Realize that for him to even say those things to you is disrespectful, and a sign that he doesn't care about your feelings. Realize that the right guy will love you flaws and all, and he won't make fun of your flaws or insult you by calling you stupid or other inappropriate names. Once you find a guy that gives you compliments instead of insults, a guy that makes you feel like the prettiest girl in the world, and a guy that wouldn't let insults about you escape from his mouth you've found Mr. Right. Let go of Mr. Verbal Abuser, and stop letting him lower your self-esteem. Your worth more than that.

A real man stands up for you and doesn't let his family disrespect you.

Mr. Mama's Boy

Mr. Mama's boy is sweet, but he can't make his own decisions. You think if you could just get his mom out of the picture everything would be great between you two. He always needs his mom's opinion or approval for everything. You will feel as if you're competing with his mom for his attention, and that you have to win his mom over just to get him to love you. If you meet his mom and she doesn't like you he won't think you're the one for him. He takes his mom's side in every argument or dispute that you have with her. You will feel as if you're in a relationship with him and his mom. Mama's boy lets his mom know all of the relationship problems, and she's always trying to tell him how to solve them. What you need to realize is that if his mother hates you it's probably because he has told her some bad things about you. He tells her everything thing that you do wrong that's why she dislikes you, and no matter how nice you are to her she will only believe what her son has said about you. Mama's boy will claim that he doesn't know why his mom dislikes you, but he knows why, and it's because of what he's said to her about you. Have you ever had a friend or relative tell you something bad about their boyfriend, and you hated their boyfriend without even knowing him? That's exactly what's happening when his relatives or friends hate you without knowing anything about you. Well, at least what you've told them about you. Mama's boy refuses to stand up to his mom on your behalf, and he always chooses his mom over you. Realize that you'll never be able to compete with his mom because she is an important part of his life, and he lives his life to please her. He needs his mom's approval to feel good about himself, and he loves when his mom praises him. If he introduces you to his mom and she doesn't approve of you or praise him you're out the door. If he doesn't leave you because of his mom's opinion of you tell the Mamas boy that you want your relationship problems to remain in the relationship, and that his mom has to stay out of your arguments. Also, tell him that you want him to stand up for you, and tell his mom not to disrespect you. If he continues to run to her, and let her control the relationship realize that he's Mr. Wrong. If he were right for you, he would stand up to his mom and have your back sometimes too. Never stay with a man that can't make decisions without his mother's approval. That's a sign that he isn't mature enough or responsible enough to be in a relationship. Realize that you need a real man, not a boy that can't make decisions without his mother's approval.

Holding onto a man that wants to sleep with you, but not be with you is settling for less.

Mr. Friend with Benefits

This guy starts off as your friend or someone you're dating, but eventually he stops taking you on romantic dates, and just wants to hang out with you. He stops romancing you or taking you on dates because he realizes that he's not into you, and he doesn't think you're the one. If you're dating a guy and his whole attitude towards you changes, and he stops taking you out pay extra attention to him because that's a sign that he's switching you from potential girlfriend to friends with benefits. A guy that's interested in you will continue to take you on romantic dates, and take you to places where couples go. A guy that has lost interest in you will only want to hang out at your place or his place or at places that aren't romantic or for couples. Some men only romance women they have romantic feelings for. Another sign is that he'll stop trying to get to know you, and he'll stop asking you questions about yourself. He stops because he only wants a physical or sexual connection with you not an emotional or mental connection. At the beginning of any type of relationship or involvement with a guy tell him you're not looking for a casual relationship. Also, make sure the guy you're interested in profile says that he's looking for a relationship as well. Never get involved with a guy that isn't looking for a relationship or commitment. Some women get involved with men with 'not looking' on their profile hoping that they can change his mind. Doing that is signing up for Mr. Wrong. Some Mr. Friends with benefits lead you on, and some will make it crystal clear that that's all that you are. This section will go over the ones that lead you on. Most Friends with Benefits know the woman has feelings for them, but they play into it or go along with it because they want sex from them. If you know someone has feelings for you, and you continue to take from them knowing that you're not interested in them you're using them. However, you don't care that you're using them because you only care about getting your needs met. Mr. Friends with Benefits knows that the only reason you're having sex with him is because you have feelings for him. Yet, he continues to sleep with you even though he doesn't plan on ever being with you. Now, some 'Friends with Benefits' actually step up to the plate, and commit, but those are rare. If you think your Friends with Benefits doesn't know that you have feelings for him think again. He knows you do, but most Mr. Wrongs hope that you won't say anything, and that things will stay the same. Most men dread the day when their friends with benefits asks for more or tells them that they have feelings for them because they don't want to lose their friend with benefit arrangement. Mr. Friends with Benefits acts like he's your boyfriend, and he spends a lot of time with you. However, you should realize that the time he spends with you is just something to do before having sex with you. This guy likes a lot of things about you, but he doesn't think you're the girl that he wants to spend the rest of his life with. Every guy has an image of what his dream woman looks like, and acts like in his head. If you don't match the image in his head, he won't think you're the one. Most of the time this image is unrealistic, but some guys think they'll find a woman like that one day so they remain single until they find her. Some men think they've already found the one, but something is keeping them from being her. Usually, the girl they're into isn't into them, and she has friend zoned them. However, he will still wait for her, and remain single because he thinks he'll get to be with her one day. No matter who he dates or how great a woman he finds his heart will be taken by this woman until he realizes that he'll never be with her. Mr. Friends with Benefits will confuse you because you will feel as if you're in a relationship with him even though he's not committed to you. He might even act jealous when you talk about other men or when he thinks you're interested in someone else. However, you need to realize that he's only acting jealous because he doesn't want another guy to sleep with you. Some men are territorial and they don't like sharing their women with other men. This Mr. Wrong will sleep with other women, but he won't want you to sleep with other men. He thinks his sex isn't that good if you need another man to have sex with besides him. Don't let his jealousy fool you. If he really wanted you to himself he would commit to you, and make it official. The only thing he wants to himself is what's in-between your legs. Mr. Friends with Benefits is attracted to you, and he enjoys your company, but that doesn't mean that he wants to commit to you. Just because a guy is attracted to you physically, and enjoys you sexually it doesn't mean that he wants to commit to you emotionally. A guy can love your good sex, but still not love you. When you're with this guy you'll notice that he isn't taking care of your emotional needs. The reason he isn't is because he's not there to be your boyfriend he's there to be your friend with benefits. Basically, leave your emotions at the door because he's just looking for company, and someone to have sex with. To a guy a friends with benefits relationship is perfect because they can have a girl on call to take care of their sexual needs, and they don't have to commit to her. Some girls actually take care of their friends with benefits. They cook, clean, and help him out with his problems. Basically, they act like they're in a relationship with him. He loves it because he gets everything he wants from you with no commitment, and he doesn't have to answer to you. He doesn't have to tell you where's he's going or where he's been. Plus, he can still talk to other women, and you can't say anything about it because he's still single. Don't be fooled, just because he acts like your boyfriend it doesn't mean he is your boyfriend. This guy is still searching for Mrs. Right, and he will leave you as soon as he finds someone he is interested in. If he leaves you chances are he's found someone to replace you with. Sometimes he leaves you for another friends with benefits, and sometimes he leaves you and jumps into a relationship. If that relationship fails or he doesn't have another friend with benefits he will come back to you. You might be giving him sex, money, attention, company, and anything else that he wants without a commitment. He doesn't take you seriously, and he only sees you as someone that is temporary. Someone to pass time with, do things with, and have sex with. Basically, you're like a girlfriend that he doesn't have to answer to, commit to or help out with. He doesn't have to do anything besides have sex with you, and that's why he sticks around for so long. He doesn't have to help you with your problems, listen to your problems, be there for you or do anything for you. After a while most women want more because they're unhappy, and the reason that they're unhappy is because Mr. Friends with Benefits isn't taking care of their emotional needs. Also, they realize that things aren't progressing, and it doesn't seem like he wants things to progress. They might feel used, played or other things, but since they enjoy his company and sex they hold onto him. Most women hold onto this Mr. Wrong because they have great chemistry with him in the bedroom, and they get along with him. After most women spend a lot of time with a man, and have sex with him they begin to have feelings for him. However, some women think they're in love with their friend with benefits, but they're not. If he asked them to marry him they would probably say 'NO'. If you have a friends with benefits do you want to marry him? Is he the type of guy that you want to marry, and have a family with? If not, you're not in love with him you're just seeking validation. This Mr. Wrong refuses to commit to you, and that makes you feel like you're not good enough. You think something must be wrong with you, and that's why he won't commit to you. So, you try to change yourself, and you try to do whatever you can to prove to him that you would be a good wife or girlfriend to him. You're constantly thinking of ways that you can make him fall in love with you, However, the longer he goes without committing to you the more worthless you feel. Realize that a guy refusing to commit to you is a sign that he's Mr. Wrong. If it has been over 6 months, and all you do with him is have sex, and he still calls you a friend. Move on because you're settling for less. Mr. Friends with Benefits is usually good in bed, and you two might have great chemistry in the bedroom. Some women think that the good sex is a sign that he could be the right guy for them. They feel close to him during sex, and unlike Mr. Booty Call, Mr. Friends with Benefits will act more romantic in the bedroom. He does this because he wants to kiss, and be close to a woman sexually. Some women confuse this physical closeness, and lust for her body as an emotional attachment. Realize that when you have sex with Mr. Wrong he only wants to connect with you on a physical level not an emotional level. Never have sex with a man to try to connect with him emotionally. The only time a guy will connect emotionally with you during sex is if he's in love with you. Never confuse Mr. Friends with Benefits kissing and other things he does in the bedroom as a sign that he wants more from you. If he wanted more from you, he would connect with you outside of the bedroom too, and he would connect with you on an emotional level not just a sexual level. His sex might be good, but if that's all he's offering you that's all he thinks your worth. Is the good sex worth disrespecting yourself for? If so, keep doing it, but if you want more from a guy than just good sex move on. To let go of this Mr. Wrong you have to stand up for yourself, and confront him. Tell him you want more, and that you're looking for a relationship not Friends with Benefits. If he's into you he'll step up to the plate. If he's not into you he'll make up an excuse for why he can't be with you or he'll slowly vanish out of your life. Never be afraid to tell a guy how you feel. If you tell him how you feel, and he doesn't feel the same way that you do he's wrong for you. Also, you have the right to know where you stand with him. If he wants to sleep with you, and enjoy everything that you have to offer he should step up to the plate. If he doesn't think you're good enough to be with you shouldn't think he's good enough to sleep with. Letting a man that doesn't even want to claim you as his girlfriend enjoy your body is settling for less. It should make you mad that someone that calls themselves your friend only wants you around for sex. It should make you mad that someone that calls themselves your friend uses you for sex knowing that they don't want to be with you. Mr. Friends with Benefits isn't your friend he's just a guy that's sleeping with you, taking everything you've got, and refusing to commit to you. You hold onto him because you think that always being there for him, supporting him, giving him good sex, cooking for him, and making him happy will make him fall in love with you. You think that one day he'll look at you, and realize that you're the one for him. However, you should realize that if it has been over 6 months, you haven't met his parents, he's never there for you, he never takes you on romantic dates, and he refuses to claim you as more than friends that he's not into you. Mr. Friends with Benefits vanishes on Holidays, Valentine's Day, and your birthday. Usually, he doesn't give you a gift or celebrate holidays with you. That should be a big red flag to you of where you stand with him. If it's your birthday and you don't even get a card, and he just sends you a text you're not important to this guy. A text for your birthday or holidays isn't what you want. You want someone to spend the holidays with, but you won't find a guy to spend Valentine's Day, Christmas or your birthday with until you let go of Mr. Friend with Benefits. If he were your friend he wouldn't do things that he knows would hurt you, and he wouldn't want you to be played or used by someone. The fact that he's the one that's using you or playing you makes it worse. If you want more don't settle for this type of treatment. If you take away the sex what else do you have with him? If nothing, you know where you stand. If dick is the only thing he's offering you, then you know where you stand. It sounds mean, but that's because it's true, and the truth hurts. If he wanted to be with you, he would be with you, no excuses. Don't think you're not good enough or that something must be wrong with you. Just realize that he's Mr. Wrong. The right guy will think you're more than good enough. The right guy will get on his knees one day, and ask you to be his wife. Mr. Friends with Benefits won't even ask you to be his girlfriend so don't think he'll ask you to be his wife. This Mr. Wrong is stopping you from meeting the right guy. Most women are single because they're being faithful, and loyal to a guy that doesn't even claim them as more than friends. You think it's right that your so called friend, has sex with you, spends time with you, and takes everything he can from you, and then has the audacity to say that you're just his friend. Since when did friends do everything that couples do? Well, these days most people want all of the benefits of a relationship without the commitment. You're giving a friend relationship benefits. From now on never give a friend all the benefits of being in a relationship with you. If you're just his friend you shouldn't be acting like his wife or his girlfriend. Find a guy that wants all of you, not parts of you. Be with a guy that wants to connect with you emotionally, mentally and sexually not just sexually. Let go of Mr. Friends with Benefits, and stopping letting your so called 'friend' use you for sex.

How to avoid 'friends with benefits?'

The only way is to wait until he commits to you to have sex with him. Not waiting can get you put into this category.

Will waiting for sex make a guy commit to you?

No, if a guy isn't interested in you, you can make him wait 100 years, and he still won't be interested in you. However, waiting until a guy commits to you stops you from getting used by players who don't plan on committing or being with you. Also, making a guy wait for sex makes him respect you more.

If you're a nice girl you should be someone's girlfriend or wife, not someone's side chick, booty call, one-night stand or Friends with Benefits. Know your worth.

Mr. Booty Call

Mr. Booty Call is similar to Mr. Friends with Benefits, but he's more disrespectful, and he doesn't try to hide the fact that he's not into you. Usually, he calls you late at night or close to the weekend to setup a time when you two can meet up. Usually, the only place you will hang out with him at is unromantic places and your place or his place. Mr. Booty Call will hang out with you just to have sex with you. After you give him sex he makes you leave his place or he leaves your place. After you have sex with him you will feel used because that's exactly what he's doing to you. He's using you for sex. You're just someone for him to release his sperm into, and get off. He doesn't respect you, and he doesn't think you're the one. If he does stay the night, he'll leave as soon as he wakes up or he'll make you leave his place before morning. Mr. Booty Call only sees you as a number in his phone, a number he can call when he wants to get laid. He will call to set up last minute plans because his other booty calls weren't available. He will call after the club because he didn't find a girl at the club to go home with. He never takes you on Romantic dates. He doesn't care about your problems, and he doesn't try to get to know you. Conversations with this guy are usually one-sided. You will have to keep the conversations going because he really doesn't want to talk to you. He'll only text you or call you when he wants to ask you to come over or meet up. Other than that you have to call or text him or you won't hear from him. He never calls or texts you first because he doesn't care about you or getting to know you. You're just sex to him, and he doesn't try to hide it. It's obvious that sex is all he wants, but you think that being there for him or giving him good sex will win him over. You think that good sex will make him fall in love with you or that you can prove that you're good enough to be his girlfriend. Realize that this guy only sees you as someone to have sex with. He doesn't think you're the one, and he doesn't even respect you. If he leaves as soon as sex is over he doesn't even want to cuddle with you or stay the night with you, he just wants to get away from you. Realize that this guy will hang out with you before sex just to get you in the mood to have sex. He might cuddle with you or watch a movie with you before sex to get you in the mood, but after sex, he leaves. If your booty call just comes over, has sex and then leaves he doesn't even think you're good enough to spend time with. Once he leaves he doesn't call or text you first again until he wants to make plans to meet up again. Basically, you're like a free prostitute to him, someone he can call whenever he wants to have sex. The right guy will cuddle with you after sex because he wants to hold you. Some men hate cuddling, but they still do it if they're into you, and they know you like it. The right guy will make love to you, and he'll want to be with you. The right guy will want all of you not just your body, and he'll stay with you for life not just for a night. Let go of Mr. Booty Call, and stop letting him treat you like a whore. You're worth more than that.

When a cheater says he won't cheat on you again he really means "I slipped, but next time you won't catch me.

If your man was the 'faithful' type you wouldn't have to worry about other women.

Mr. Cheater

Mr. Cheater committed to you because he wanted to take you off the market. He doesn't want another man to have you or sleep with you. He doesn't respect you, but he thinks he's in love with you. The reason I say 'think' is because if he loved you he wouldn't be disrespecting you, and doing things that would make him lose you. Mr. Cheater wants to live like a single man, but he also wants a family of his own. He wants the wife, the kids, and the picket fence, but he doesn't want the commitment. In fact, he doesn't even think cheating is that bad of a thing? He sees the other women as sex objects, but he sees you as someone that is different from other women. He sees you as someone he can spend the rest of his life with, and be in a long term open relationship with. Of course, it will only be open on his end, because he wants you to be the faithful, loyal wife while he goes out and dates who he wants. He thinks all men cheat on their wife or girlfriend and that it's normal for a man to cheat. Mr. Cheater doesn't go out looking for women to replace you with, he goes out looking for women he can have sex with. Since it's only sex to him, and he doesn't have feelings for these women he doesn't see cheating as something that should hurt you. You might catch him saying things like 'it's not that big of a deal' or 'it was just sex' or 'she didn't mean anything to me'. One woman isn't good enough for him. The more women he can sleep with the better. He thinks that one woman can't satisfy all of his needs or wants. He lacks self-control, and he's unfaithful, but he wants you to be faithful. If he cheats he wants you to forgive him, and take him back. If you were to cheat he'd think of you as a whore who doesn't deserve a second chance. He cheats on you, but he doesn't want you to cheat on him because he knows cheating is wrong. Basically, he wants you to treat him right, but he doesn't treat you right. Mr. Cheater is the King of Double Standards. You might even hear him say things like 'it's okay for men to sleep around or have multiple women, but a woman shouldn't'. He expects a lot from you, but he doesn't give you the same things back. He can hang out with his friends all night, but if you go out with your girlfriends and stay out too long he will blow your phone up with nonstop calls. He does this because he doesn't trust you, and the reason he doesn't trust you is because he thinks you might cheat on him too. After a while, Mr. Cheater will start accusing you of all sorts of things, and usually it's things he's doing himself. When you catch Mr. Cheater cheating on you, he will give you an excuse for why he cheated, and blame you for his actions. Or he will try to turn the tables on you and accuse you of being unfaithful too. Or he might even blame the other woman, and say she's crazy, and that she won't leave him alone. No matter what he says to you there's no excuse for cheating. Also, it's his job to be faithful, and turn down women that pursue him. If you're with a man that can't control his actions or turn down other women be prepared to get cheated on a lot. Some women who have unfaithful partners like blaming the other woman because they want an excuse to give their man another chance. They act as if their man didn't have any part of what happened, and that he was seduced by the other woman. Chances are the other woman didn't know he was taken, and she is getting played too. However, Mr. Cheater will just step back, and let her take the blame for his actions because he doesn't want his partner to leave him. When Mr. Cheater cheats he gives himself an excuse for why he should be allowed to cheat. The excuse he gives himself makes him feel better about his actions, and usually, the excuse is something he blames on you. He will tell himself that you're cheating on him too and that he has the right to cheat on you back. He will tell himself that he has the right to cheat on you because you're never home or because you're not taking care of his sexual needs. Whatever his excuse is he believes that it justifies his actions. Whenever you catch him cheating he will throw this excuse in your face and expect you to feel sorry for him or take the blame for his actions. Mr. Cheater likes sneaking around. He enjoys the double life, the challenge of keeping the secret from you, playing as many women as he can, and trying to get away with it. If he sees a woman he's attracted to, and he has the opportunity to sleep with her he will. Basically, you're in a relationship with a single man that is playing house. He wants the American dream of being in a loving family, but he also wants the freedom that single life brings. So, he tries to balance the two because he's not the type of man that is capable of settling down with one woman. Realize that Mr. Cheater is putting your health at risk. He's sleeping with other women and coming back home to your bed. Leave before he brings you home something you can't get rid of. Some people with HIV got it because their spouse or partner cheated on them with prostitutes or other women that are infected with HIV. Realize that Mr. Cheater isn't worth ruining your health for, and if he loved you he wouldn't be out there sleeping with other women. Mr. Cheater puts his sexual wants before your emotional needs. In other words, he chooses sex with other women over your feelings. His sexual desires control him, and he likes to have a variety of women at his disposal. Usually, he has different women taking care of different things for him, and he uses the other women to escape from his married or taken life. The other women provide a fake life for him to escape to; a life with no problems or drama, and lots of sex. This Mr. Wrong loves having multiple women giving him love and affection. Having multiple women gives him an ego boost. It makes him feel like a real man, and he likes the drama. If both women fight over him he loves it even more. When two women fight over him he feels special, and he sees it as a challenge. Since he wants to keep both women he tells both women that he's leaving the other woman or that the other woman won't leave him alone. He tells each woman what they want to hear, and makes them feel like he is choosing them over the other woman. However, he just wants to keep both women in his life. If his plans and sweet words work, and he gets to keep both of you his ego soars through the roof. After he apologizes, says sweet words, and promises to change you might take him back hoping that he'll change. Then he'll act really sweet for a while, pretending like he has changed then he starts cheating again. He cheats, apologizes then you take him back. This cycle will repeat until you realize your worth, and you realize that you deserve better. You'll leave because you're tired of looking stupid or foolish, and you're sick of sharing your man with other women. You'll also leave because you'll finally realize that he will never change and that he's not the type of man that you're looking for. The type of man you're looking for is a man that will be faithful to you. A man that respects his partner, and knows how to keep his penis in his pants. Let go of Mr. Cheater, and stop letting him put your health at risk. Stop letting him play you, play house, and have his cake and eat it too. You deserve better than that.

If he's your man tell me why he's still chasing other women? His actions prove that he isn't committed to you or the relationship.

Some women brag about sleeping with another woman's man like being the side chick is something special. Realize that being the side chick is nothing to brag about.

Mr. Taken

When you first meet this guy he pretends like he's single or he pretends as if he's in the middle of a divorce or he pretends like he's leaving his girlfriend soon. If he's the type that pretends like he's single red flags will pop up immediately. The biggest red flag is that he will control when you two talk. He does this because he is always around his woman, and he can't answer your calls when he's around her. He will have times where he disappears and doesn't answer your calls or text. Usually, it's at night or holidays when he disappears, but you'll notice a pattern with him. There will be times when you know he isn't at work, and that he should be available but he isn't. He will call you when he's out for a drive or out somewhere. He will also call you around the same time every day because that's the time when he isn't around his woman. Usually, when he's at work or she's at work is the best time for him to contact you. He will hang up the phone on you or rush to end a call out of nowhere because his woman has come home or is approaching him. Mr. Taken won't spend holidays with you because that's family and wife/girlfriend time. Mr. Taken will barely answer your calls because he's around her, but when he can sneak away from her he'll call you back. Or when you call he'll send you a quick text, to stop you from calling again. Mr. Taken will stand you up a lot or meet you at places that or out of town or places that his girlfriend/wife never goes. If Mr. Taken has told you that he's in the middle of a divorce or he's leaving his girlfriend soon move on immediately. Never start a relationship with a man that isn't 100% done with his current relationship. If you do you might get played, and you're also disrespecting his wife/girlfriend. Chances are Mr. Taken isn't getting a divorce or leaving his girlfriend. He just tells you that because he wants to sleep with you and make you feel as if he'll leave her for you. This Mr. Wrongs first game is to try to make you feel sorry for him. He tells you that his current relationship makes him unhappy, that his woman is mean to him or crazy, and that she doesn't treat him right. You will feel sorry for him, and you will believe the things he says about his current partner because he doesn't seem like that bad of a guy to you. However, you should realize that a guy that is trying to cheat on his partner with you isn't a decent guy at all. If his partner was as bad as he claims he would have already left her. Some Mr. Taken's will tell you that they're staying with their kid's mom because of the kids, but they're not with her. If you believe that a man is staying with the mother of his kids, and he's not sleeping with her you're naive. I'm not trying to be mean, but that's an obvious lie, and if you stay with him he's going to play you like there's no tomorrow. He knows that if you fell for that lie you'll fall for anything else he tells you. Never stay with a man that is living with another woman that he dated previously. That's the biggest red flag ever. Whenever you ask Mr. Taken when he's going to leave or when will the divorce be final he always extends the time, and tells you to wait a little bit longer. Some Mr. Taken's actually leave their wife for their mistress, but that's rare. Usually, Mr. Taken cuts off the mistress after his wife/girlfriend finds out about her. Mr. Taken doesn't want to lose his current relationship, and if he has to cut you off to keep his partner he will. However, the first thing he does is try to keep both the Mistress and the partner. He'll tell his partner that he cut off the mistress, and tell the mistress that he's leaving his wife soon. Sometimes he'll cut off one mistress, behave for a while, and then find a new mistress. Mr. Taken likes living a double life. It makes him feel important, and special because he has 2 women that need him or wants him. Know your worth, and find a man that isn't already taken. You shouldn't want to sleep with a man that goes home to sleep with his wife or girlfriend. The same sweet words he says to you he says to his wife or girlfriend. He keeps you a secret, and he doesn't make you a part of his life. Never stay with a man that keeps you a secret. A man that already belongs to another woman isn't the type of man you want to settle down with. If you settle down with him chances are you'll be the wife that gets cheated on next. As the old saying goes "If he cheats with you, he'll cheat on you. If he tells you that he's in the middle of a divorce or he's leaving his girlfriend soon tell him to call you when he has his divorce papers or when he moves out and gets a place of his own. Chances are you'll never get that call or see those divorce papers or see him move out of the home he shares with his partner. Realize that you should be with a man that you don't have to share. A man that would choose you over other women. Some women like being the side chick because it makes them feel special and powerful. They think that seducing a taken man and stealing him from his wife is fun and a challenge. They think that if he sleeps with them that they're better than his wife or girlfriend. You might catch them bragging about sleeping with another woman's man or how they can take your man if they wanted too. If you're this type of woman realize that sleeping with another woman's man isn't anything to brag about. Doing that makes you a side chick, and being a side chick isn't anything to brag about. In the end, he married her, and you're just someone that he sleeps with. Both of you should realize your worth and let go of Mr. Taken because he's playing you both. Instead of fighting each other you both need to team up, and drop him. The main reason you dislike each other is because you both want a no good, two timing man that is lying to you both. Wake up ladies, and stop looking dumb for a sorry man. Let go of Mr. Taken, and stop being his side piece of meat that he keeps a secret. You're worth more than that.

A relationship built on lies will fall apart when the truth comes out.

Mr. Liar

When you first meet Mr. Liar he'll seem like your dream guy. Everything he says is sweet, and he seems genuinely interested in you. He tells you that he wants to take you to places and that he wants to do special things for you. However, you'll soon realize that he isn't doing any of the things he promised. Usually, he starts off with small lies like he'll call you back later, but then he doesn't call you back until the next day or days later. He will make plans with you, and not show up. He will cancel dates at the last minute, and give you a dumb excuse for why he has to cancel. He might tell you that he has a car, but later on you find out he doesn't have one. He might tell you he doesn't have kids, but later on, you find out he has quite a few. This guy lies about everything, but you stay because when he does deliver on his promise you enjoy the time that he spends with you. However, he has stood you up plenty of times. He knew he had plans with you, he knew you'd get ready, and he knew he wasn't coming. He just didn't' care about his promise to you, and he decided to do something else instead. He doesn't respect you or your time. He thinks he has you wrapped around his finger, and he can make you wait on him. Chances are you're too available, and you're always available to do what he wants to do whenever he wants to do it. You also keep giving him chances after chances even though he continues to flake on you. Basically, he doesn't think you're going anywhere. When he doesn't show up he's already planning what he'll say to you, and he knows it will work on you because you fall for his sweet talk or you fall for his sob stories. Unless he had a death in his family or a life-threatening emergency he should have at least called to cancel. When he tells you lies it makes him feel good. Promising you things makes him feel like he's a good person, and that he's trying. However, he doesn't deliver on his promises because he isn't capable or he doesn't want to. Some men flake or cancel last minute dates that are expensive because they're broke or low on cash. If you think that might be the case suggest something free or less expensive for you two to do. Just make sure it isn't at your place or his. A walk in the park, the beach, ice cream, or Starbucks are less expensive ideas. If he declines your free options then he is just planning to do something else, and he is canceling you at the last minute for other reasons. Words are just words to Mr. Liar, and he doesn't take himself seriously. He promises things thinking that he might be able to deliver, but if he can't deliver or doesn't want to deliver he avoids you instead of just telling you or canceling you. Basically, he's a coward, and telling you that he can't be there or do something he promised makes him feel like less of a man, and it makes him feel like he isn't as great as he pretends to be. To avoid feeling like he let you down or like he's not as great as he pretends to be he just avoids you and stands you up. However, when he thinks he can deliver he comes back to you or calls you, and tries to make it up to you. When you catch Mr. Liar lying he will tell you another lie to try to cover that one up or he'll tell you a sob story so you'll feel sorry for him. Sometimes he'll ignore your calls when you're trying to see if he's still coming because he's too scared to cancel. If you just met a guy, and he's already lying and standing you up move on. His behavior will get worse, and you'll never know when he'll show up or not. Or if he will deliver on his promises or words to you. Basically, his words are sweet, but his actions are quite the opposite. He'll plan a nice romantic date, and you'll be excited about it, but then he'll stand you up or cancel it at the last minute. You might like this guy, but he's not responsible, and he's untrustworthy. A real man is honest, and he doesn't stand you up for dates. If a real man says he'll be there he'll be there, and if he can't make it you'll be the first one to know. Plus, he'll say he'll make it up to you, and he will make it up to you. Also, he'll feel bad for not being able to make it, and he'll apologize once or twice because he cares about your feelings. Mr. Liar doesn't care about your feelings that's why he lies to you, cancels things at the last minute, and doesn't seem to care about what he did. If he apologizes you'll know it's not sincere because he will do it again and again until you get sick and tired of his lies. You'll catch him lying about things he doesn't even have to lie about. He'll tell you stories that seem made up and fake. When he's telling you lies you'll smell the bullshit. He'll tell you he's rich, and he'll even lie about his occupation. This guy is just a walking lie, and he lives in a fantasy world that he has created for himself. He doesn't think you'll like him if you know the truth about him so he pretends to be someone he isn't or he pretends that he can do things that he isn't' capable of doing. For example; he works at a minimum wage job, but he pretends to be a Lawyer or a Doctor. However, you can tell that he doesn't have the money that a Doctor or Lawyer has. Or he will tell you that he has a car, but it's being repaired at the moment, and you never see that car. Mr. Liar tells you anything just to keep you around. Realize that his promises and words might be sweet, but he'll barely follow through. Women put up with Mr. Liar because he seems like a nice guy who means well, and they enjoy his company. However, they need to realize that Mr. Liar will never change, and he isn't the type of man you want to marry. If you have kids with this type of Mr. Wrong he will lie to them, and stand them up too. In the future, when he stands your kids up and lies to them you'll realize that he's doing the same thing to them that he did to you. Let go of Mr. Wrong, and stop believing or falling for his lies. Actually, you don't believe his lies you just ignore them because you think he'll change one day, and you think he'll start doing what he's supposed to do. If you confront Mr. Liar about his lies and broken promises he will get defensive because he hates people telling him the truth about himself. The liar hates hearing the truth and telling the truth. When you're confronting him he feels out of control, and his ego feels threatened. Chances are he'll leave the conversation, or leave the room or give you the silent treatment. Mr. Liar lives in a made up fantasy world where he's a great guy, and he hates when people say otherwise.

Realize that you'll never make an honest person out of a liar. Realize that you deserve someone that will be honest with you. Someone that you can trust, and someone that want lie to your kids or future kids. Don't fall for sweet words. When you first meet Mr. Wrong he will say all kinds of sweet things to you, and those things will make you smile. However, you shouldn't get too mushy over his words because he doesn't even know you yet, and if he doesn't know you yet he's in lust with you not in love with you. Listen to his words, but don't get happy until he actually shows you how he feels about you. Let go of Mr. Wrong, and stop waiting around for a sorry excuse of a man that you don't even trust. Trust is the most important part of a relationship, and you'll never be able to trust Mr. Liar. Realize you're worth more than that.

A man that's isn't' trying to connect with you emotionally or mentally, but is trying to rush you into sexual things isn't into you.

Mr. Hoe

Doesn't keep what he wants hidden. He will have pictures of himself displaying his penis through his shorts, speedos, boxers or towel. He will have sexual comments in his dating profile and brag about his bedroom skills. On the first date, he will try to feel on you, and try to rush things to test how far you are willing to go. In instant messages, he will give you compliment after compliment on your body. He'll ask you for picture after picture hoping to get a sexual one of you or he'll just ask you to send him something sexy. Also, he will talk about sex all the time, and try to change every conversation into something about sex. For example; you say you're going to bed, and he'll ask if he can join you. That would be fine if he were your partner, but it's inappropriate coming from a man you just met, and don't even know. This guy is the type of guy that only wants one thing. You'll know when you meet this guy because he won't' try to get to know you, but he will try to get you in bed, and try to get to know every inch of your body. He'll brag about his sex skills, and tell you things he would do to you. He's very disrespectful, and you should always leave a guy that isn't trying to get to know you and is always talking about what he'll do to you. His sexual talk should make you mad. I don't care how hot he is, he is disrespecting you, and treating you like a sex object. If he's naked in his dating profile showing the world his penis move on because he's sending those pics out to every woman he meets to try to get her in bed. If he sends you a penis picture out of nowhere cut him off immediately. Never talk about sex with a guy you're getting to know. Keep the conversations about other things. Let a guy get to know who you are, and your personality. If you have sex too fast you don't give him a chance to get to know you or connect with you emotionally. If a guy never connects with you emotionally, he'll put you in the friend with benefits, side chick or booty call category because that's all he ever got to know about you. You might be attracted to him, but if you're looking for a relationship move on. Just because he looks good it doesn't mean that he's a good person. He's a disrespectful guy that just so happens to be handsome too. I don't care how good a guy looks you should never let him play you. Mr. Hoe is usually full of himself, and he thinks he can have any woman he wants. Don't throw yourself at a man just because he looks good. Find a guy you're attracted to that isn't disrespectful. Don't lower your self-respect just to sleep with a man hoe. Don't think you're special just because he wants to sleep with you. He'll say sweet things to any woman with a vagina just to get laid. If you sleep with him you're just going to be another notch on his bedpost, and just another number or name on his list. You need a guy that wants to get to know you. A guy that compliments your face pictures, as much as he does your full body pictures. A guy that wants to know your dreams, your hobbies and everything else about you. This Mr. Wrong only wants you for your body, and he isn't hiding that from you. Some women try to change the subject or try to make him try to get to know them. However, if things aren't moving fast enough for him or you refuse to go along with his sexual desires, and you keep talking about yourself he ends the conversation. If he feels as if you're looking for more than what he's looking for he'll start pulling away from you. If a guy doesn't try to get to know you, and he's rushing you into bed move on. Let go of Mr. Sex, and don't give him what he wants from you. Realize that you're a woman, not a sex object.

A man that never takes responsibility for his actions isn't responsible enough or mature enough to settle down with

Mr. Blame

When you first meet this guy he will give you a laundry list of sob stories. If you listen to his stories, you'll realize that all of his stories have one thing in common and that one thing is that he always blames someone else for what happened in the story. You never hear him admit to his part in anything that happened. This guy likes to be the victim, and he always acts like the world is against him. Of course, he blames his ex for ruining the relationship or acting crazy, but he'll omit the part of the story where he cheated on her and caused her to act emotional or crazy as he calls it. If you stay with Mr. Blame you will be blamed for everything he does wrong. If he hits you, cheats on you or doesn't treat you right he'll blame it on you. He wants you to apologize for your actions, but he barely ever apologizes because he thinks he's always right. He'll cheat on you, and say it's because you weren't home enough. He'll hit you, and say it's because you made him mad. When he does apologize it isn't a real apology because he doesn't actually apologize or he'll give you an excuse with the apology. Instead of saying "I apologize" he'll say "I shouldn't have done it" or "I was wrong". Instead of a real apology he'll say "I'm sorry, BUT_____". As soon as he says 'but' he's blaming what he did on you, someone else, or something else, and he isn't holding himself accountable for his actions. Never stay with someone that has too much pride to apologize to you or doesn't care about you enough to apologize for wrongdoings. If he can never admit when he's wrong the relationship will be one-sided, and you'll always have to be the one that fixes the relationship problems because he won't admit to doing anything wrong. A person that doesn't think they're wrong won't apologize to you. Now, you can stay with him and get blamed for his bad behavior or you can move on and find a guy that takes responsibility for his actions. A real man swallows his pride and apologizes for his actions. When a real man apologizes he places the blame on himself, not you. When a real man upsets you he understands why you're mad, and he says that you have the right to be mad. When Mr. Blame upsets you he acts like you're over exaggerating or like you don't have the right to be mad. He doesn't think you have the right to be mad because he blames you for what he did. He thinks that if you had treated him better that he would have behaved. When he doesn't get his way or worshiped by you, he disrespects you to pay you back, and then he says you made him act up. Stop letting a weak man who can't even admit when he's wrong play you and blame you for everything that HE does wrong. His actions are his choice, not yours. Realize that you're worth more than that.

Mr. Rebound

Whenever you meet someone you might ask them about their ex or why they ended their last relationship just to get to know more about them. However, when you meet Mr. Rebound he talks about his ex non-stop, and he even compares you to his ex. Mr. Rebound will say bad things about his ex, and then say you remind him of her. Or you'll do something and he'll say his ex used to do that too. If Mr. Rebound is really stuck on his ex he might even call you her name by mistake. This Mr. Wrong is focused on his ex, and he doesn't have room in his heart for you. If his ex broke up with him all she has to do is snap her finger, and he'll run back to her. If he broke up with her, he's trying to get over her by talking about her to you. However, this constant ex talk is a sign that he's not over his last relationship, and he's definitely not ready to start a new relationship. Giving yourself to a man that is still focused on his last relationship can lead to you getting a broken heart. If he regrets leaving her he'll go back to her, and leave you. When a guy can't stop thinking about a girl he thinks he's in love with her. Even if that girl has rejected him, hurt him or used him he still will want to be with her. A woman knows when a guy seems to be stuck on his ex. When he talks about his ex you'll see it in his eyes and in his facial expressions. You'll know that he still has feelings for her, but you'll think you can replace her, and show him that you can treat him better than how she treated him. However, if he is talking about her non-stop you should move on. If you really like him offer a friendship, and just be his friend until he gets over her. Being his friend will bring you closer to him, but it will also keep you from getting played or used if he does decide to go back to her. If you have sex with Mr. Rebound, and he goes back to his ex you'll feel used or like she's better than you. However, she isn't better than you, it's just that she had his heart way before he met you. It's okay to be this Mr. Wrongs friend, but don't be more than that until he moves on. Realize that you're the only girl your man should be talking about non-stop. If he's talking about his ex non-stop then he's Mr. Wrong NOT Mr. Right.

Mr. Broken Hearted Player

When you meet this guy he will tell you a sob story about how his ex broke his heart. Usually, this ex broke up with him or cheated on him a long time ago, but he still isn't over it. You will feel sorry for him, and you'll give him all of your love because you want to fix his broken heart. After you hear his sob story you make it your mission to be the woman you feel he needs in his life. He will act like his ex was the most horrible person on the planet. You'll also get the feeling that he still isn't over her, and guess what you're right. Mr. Broken Hearted Player isn't over the ex who broke his heart, and even if he gives you a chance he will always wonder about the girl who got away, hurt him or left him. Also, Mr. Broken Hearted Player doesn't trust women. The girl who broke his heart left him with trust issues. He is constantly thinking that a woman is trying to play him or is going to play him. His guard is always up, and if he thinks a woman is out to get him he begins to play games. Basically, he wants to leave you, hurt you or play you before you can play him. He's afraid to get hurt again. So, he puts walls around his heart to protect himself from getting hurt again. He plays games because he thinks women are going to play him. Every time you don't answer his text or respond to his calls he panics and begins to think you're fixing to be like the women in his past. Mr. Broken hearted Player is broken, and you'll make it your mission to try to fix him. However, you should realize that he has to fix himself. He has to fix his own trust issues, and he has to be willing to give love another chance. If you stay with him he's only going to play you because he doesn't trust you. The only thing he's thinking about is the girl who broke his heart, and how he can stop another girl from breaking it again. One day when he's sick of being lonely, and he learns how to trust again he'll change. Until then he's just a player with a broken heart. The difference between a broken-hearted player and a regular player is that the broken hearted player plays games to protect himself from getting hurt, and the regular player plays games for fun or as a lifestyle.

Mr. Woman Hater

When you first meet this guy he'll say comments about women as if all women are the same. "You know how y'all women are", "Women are evil", "Why do women play games", and "All women are the same, but I think you're different." Basically, he'll act as if you're just like the other women he dated even though he doesn't even know you. He might even ask you to prove that you're different. This Mr. Wrong was hurt by a woman; his mom or an ex, and now he secretly hates all women. He thinks all women are the same, and that they're evil. He doesn't trust women, and as soon as you do 1 thing wrong that's enough for him to think you're playing games with him. As soon as he thinks you're playing games he begins to play games, and he doesn't take you seriously. Also, when he hurts you or plays games with you, he thinks you deserve it, and he might even enjoy hurting you. He takes the anger he feels for the women in his past out on you. Since he doesn't like women he doesn't respect them, and since he doesn't respect them he doesn't care about their feelings. He believes that all women are no good and that they deserve what's coming to them. When he plays you it makes him feel like he's gotten revenge on the women in his past. Realize that the woman hater is filled with too much hate, and if you hold onto them all of that hate is going to be directed towards you. They're going to make you pay for all the pain and suffering they feel. Mr. Woman Hater hates women, but he still wants a relationship. He just can't trust anyone enough to settle down. He's always on edge and watching his back. Until he lets go of the past and realizes that all women aren't the same he won't change. He might seem heartless, but that's far from the truth. The Woman hater is hurting inside, and he's filled with so much anger and pain. However, instead of releasing the pain in a positive way, he releases it in a negative way and takes it out on innocent women. Women who had nothing to do with what happened to him in his past. When you spot the Women Hater spewing his lies about women, and how they're all the same run because he isn't going to give you a fair chance to win his heart. He thinks he already knows you, and he thinks you're going to mistreat him even though he doesn't even know you yet.

Mr. Player

Mr. Player loves playing games. It has become a lifestyle for him. In his world the only person's feelings he cares about are his own. Women are just objects for him to play with, and their feelings don't matter to him. He will say and do whatever he has to do to get what he wants from a woman. He even practices his pick-up skills or lines that he will say to women. You will find this guy bragging about how many women he has at his disposal, and he'll usually have friends that are players too. His friends will cheer him on, and they'll have competitions to see who can get the most girls or play the best. It's a game to him and it makes him feel cool and manlier. A player usually has women chasing after him. He loves the attention, and the more women that throw themselves at him the more of a player he will become. After all, why should he settle down with one woman when 10 are chasing after him? In his mind it's better to just stay single because you don't have to help a woman with her problems or bills. Plus, you don't have to check in or tell a woman anything. He loves his lifestyle because he can sleep with whomever, whenever, and no-one can say anything about it because he's single. Some women think they can change a player, but the only person that can change him is himself. Most players don't want to change. They enjoy their lifestyle, and they don't want to give it up. They like having sex with a variety of women, they like the challenge of picking up new women, and they think they're god's gift to women. Most players use lame lies, and excuses to keep you around. The player will start off chasing you then you'll notice that he'll begin to lose interest in you or he'll pull back, and make you chase him. Next thing you know you're calling and texting him first all the time, and you only hear from him when he's bored or wants something or wants to meet up. If a guy is making you do all the calling, texting, and planning he's not that into you. You shouldn't be chasing him, and you shouldn't be doing what a man is supposed to be doing. The first sign that he's a player is that he will try to skip over the getting to know you stage.

You'll notice that he isn't trying to get to know you, and he isn't telling you a lot about himself. You'll feel as if he is rushing you to have sex. From the first date, text or call he will make sexual comments or try to touch you in a sexual way. Since getting you in bed is his mission he knows he needs to make physical contact with you as soon as possible. If you met him online he'll want to meet up fast, and he won't want to have long conversations with you. Most players want to skip the small talk, and get straight to the bedroom. A real player will shower you with compliments, and he'll keep trying to take things to second, and third base. Most players will test you to see if you're easy. They will make a sexual comment or advance to see if you will take the bait. When they test you they'll act like they're joking or they'll act like it's a compliment of some sort. If you don't take the bait they'll move on or they'll tone it down, and play the nice guy card because they realize that you're going to be more of a challenge. If you take the bait they'll assume you're easy or a hoe, and they'll become pushier or sexual. Players will seem interested in you because they'll come around a lot at first but if you pay attention you'll notice that they're trying to connect with you physically, more than emotionally. You'll also notice that he'll call you less and less as time goes on. If things are moving too slow for the player, he will move on to someone easier. However, he will still text you or call you from time to time to see if he can get you in bed. Players will call you at late hours or try to make plans with you at the last minute. You'll notice that he always makes plans with you the same day he wants to meet up or late at night. Reject men who always make last minute plans or plan things late at night. If it's 8 pm on Friday night, he shouldn't be trying to schedule a date with you. That's a sign that he's looking to get laid, and that you're an option to him. A guy that's interested in you would plan a date with you as soon as possible because he wants to make sure you'll have time for him. A player thinks he can have you at any time he wants, and he wants you to drop everything you're doing for him. Tell last minute planners that you already have plans, and that you need to know of his plans at least 2 or 3 days beforehand. If he's interested in you he'll start asking ahead of time, if he's not he'll continue to ask the day of or at the last minute. If he continues to ask at the last minute delete his number immediately because he is 100% player, and he's only after one thing. Another thing players do is call you at late hours. If the guy you're dating is always calling you at late hours tell him to stop calling you so late. Answering late night calls will get you put into the booty call category. If he's calling you at 11pm to schedule a date realize that it's not a real date, it's just a booty call. In fact, you should be mad at him for even thinking that it's okay to call you up late at night to meet up. One thing you can do is tell a guy to call you instead of text you. Then start asking him about his life, and telling him about yours. Players will go along with this at first, but if things never move to the bedroom they'll start avoiding you, they'll start ending conversations fast, and they'll slowly pull away from you. Players think that all women want them, and that all women want to get them to settle down. A player knows that you have feelings for them, but since they don't feel the same they avoid having that conversation with you. They just want to keep it friendly with benefits. Basically, they want you to give them sex or money and never pressure them into being in a relationship with you because they're not interested in being more than friends with you. The player only thinks about his wants and needs. If he has to hurt you to get his needs met then so be it. Since the player isn't connected to you emotionally, he doesn't feel any emotions for you, and he doesn't really care about your feelings. He thinks that if you're dumb enough to fall for his game that you deserve to get played. He might even laugh to himself whenever he tricks you or you fall for one of his lies. It's just a joke, and a game to him, but you're taking what you have with him seriously. You want more from him than he is willing to give you, but you keep holding onto him hoping that he'll give it to you. Chances are he knew he wasn't going to give you what you wanted when he first met you. When a guy meets you it doesn't take him long to decide what category he wants to put you in. I will discuss categories later on. The player wants things to be done on his schedule. The player doesn't care if it's 3 am, if he wants sex or something else he will try to get you in bed. Even it's 3 am He will text every number in his phone until he finds someone to satisfy his sexual needs. He'll text them 'I miss you' or 'I love you' or whatever he thinks will work to get them to let him come over. Women are just sex objects to him. He thinks having a lot of women is cool because his friends and other guys see him as an Alpha male for being able to pick up women. Some players see picking up women as a skill, art or talent. These guys call themselves pick up artist. A player doesn't care if he has to lie to a woman because he doesn't respect women. Women are just hoes, bitches and sexual objects to him. Lying to women is just a part of his lifestyle, and in his world it's perfectly normal to tell women lies to get them into bed. Some players think it's okay to get a woman drunk just so they can get her into bed. You'd be surprised at how far some players will go just to get you into bed. One thing you'll notice about a player is that everything about him seems rehearsed, like he always has an excuse for everything, and that he'll lie about the dumbest things. Almost everything he says seems to come from a corny romantic movie. You'll also notice that he'll act really interested in you when you're around him, but when you're away from him he'll act distant or uninterested. This is because when he's around you he knows he has to act interested in you to get you into bed, but when he's away from you the only thing he can do is talk to you, and there isn't a chance to get you in bed. Basically, he'll make time to have sex, but he won't make time to talk to you for a long period of time. The player's favorite line is "I'm busy" or "I've been busy". He'll say he was busy, but chances are you will see him online during his so called busy times. Also, he'll always make time for what he wants to do, but he'll never make time for what you want to do. It takes less than 30 seconds to call or text someone, and if he doesn't have 30 seconds of free time to give you then you know where you stand with him. Plus, most guys have their phone glued to them. So, he has his phone on him all day, but he can't take 30 seconds to text you or call you to chat? Don't fall for that game. If the guy you're talking to makes time to sleep with you, but he says he's too busy to call or text you he's playing you. Never stay with a guy that says he's too busy for you, but he still makes time to have sex with you. Basically, he only makes time for what he wants from you, and that's sex. Mr. Player will hit and run a chick he isn't interested in at all. If he thinks you're fun to be around he might upgrade you to friends with benefits. If he likes the sex, but he doesn't like your personality or if he isn't attracted to you he will upgrade you to booty call. Most players hate rejection. When they get rejected it damages their ego, and it makes them wonder why the girl is rejecting them. All the other girls are throwing themselves at him and here comes a girl that is rejecting him. Some players will see this as a challenge, and chase after you even harder. Some will move on to someone easier. Also, I don't recommend this because it is game playing, but playing hard to get will make the player more interested in you. However, once he catches you, you will just be another notch in his belt. The only way to play him is to not sleep with him and not play his game at all. Put a player in the friend zone and he'll be uncomfortable, and try to get out of it. Trying to make a player fall in love with you will get you played in the end because as soon as you sleep with him the power you have over him will vanish. Simply because getting you in bed was his only mission. It just took him longer to get you there than it took to get other girls, but he still got you there, and that's all that matters to him. In fact, if it was really hard to get you in bed, but he still got you in bed he will think he's the best player on the planet because he won the challenge or game. However, if you never sleep with him at all he will remain interested in you because you're the one that he can't have. Don't play games just move on and find a guy that you don't have to trick into loving you. The player brags to his friends about what he does to you and other girls. Also, they share pictures, and stories of the girls they are playing. Never send a guy a picture of you that you don't want his friends or anyone else to see. As soon as he gets it, he's sharing it with his friends. Some players even refer to the women they're dating as bitches and hoes. If that's okay with you hold onto this Mr. Wrong, but if you know your worth you shouldn't want a guy to call you his hoe or his bitch. When you're out with Mr. Player, he flirts with other women in front of you, and stares at them for long periods of time. Long enough for you to notice that he's being disrespectful. It's normal for men to stare at other women, but most men try to sneak a peek, and they don't stare for long periods of time or try to make a connection with other women in front of you. Mr. Player stands you up, flakes on you, and constantly cancels plans at the last minute. Mr. Player is a combination of a lot of the Mr. Wrongs I mentioned previously. He's not the type of guy that you would want to commit to. If you were to settle down with him during his player days he'd cheat on you. Stop letting this guy play you, and string you along. Find a guy that's ready to settle down. Mr. Player won't settle down until he gets sick of being with multiple women, he learns how to trust women, and he wants a family. Some players never settle down; as long as they have options they'll never make one woman their priority. Some women believe that a player will change once he meets one special woman, and this belief makes women try to be that special woman in a player's life. However, what's really happening is that the woman isn't changing the player, the player just met a woman that fits the image in his head of what 'the one' looks like and acts like. I know it hurts, but if he didn't want to settle down with you, he didn't think you were the one. The woman that got him to settle down fits the image of 'the one' to him. It doesn't mean that she's better than you, it just means that he thinks she's better suited for him. If he chooses her over you don't think she's better than you just realize that he was the wrong guy for you. If he were Mr. Right he would have chosen you over her. When you meet the right guy he won't play you, and you'll fit the image of 'the one' that he has ingrained into his head. No-one likes to be rejected, but realize that rejection is a sign that you're trying to be with someone that you're not meant to be with.

HOW TO PLAY A PLAYER?

Don't play games just move on to someone else. Playing games back and forth with a player is a waste of time. Time that could be spent on someone that actually cares about you. However, realize that playing hard to get in bed or making a guy wait for sex won't make him fall in love with you, but it will make some players chase after you. Not because they want you, but because they think it will be a challenge to get you into bed. One thing that does work is getting close to a guy emotionally and becoming his friend first. Then once he's interested in you put him into the friend zone, and act like you're not interested in him. This works on men who can't handle rejection, but realize that they will only chase you for validation not because they love you. It's common knowledge that people chase people that ignore them or don't want them because they can't handle rejection. You should want someone to chase you because they love you not because you're playing a game. However, putting him in the friend zone and getting to know him works because once he connects with you emotionally he won't think of you as just a booty call or sex object because he has gotten to know the real you. If a guy never gets to know the real you, it's easy for him to have sex with you, and not want anything more from you. Most men aren't intrigued by women who withhold sex they're intrigued by women who withhold their emotions from them. Not being available to him emotionally or sexually, and only giving him small amounts of attention can make a player interested in you. However, playing games with a player just to get him interested in you only works temporarily. If he catches you, and he realizes that his feelings for you aren't real he will lose interest in you. Don't become a player just to get a player.

Mr. Narc

When you first meet this guy his online pictures will come off as conceited. In this guy's mind, he is the man of all men, and he is a superstar. This guy's ego is inflated beyond what it should be. He wants women to worship him, and he loves women that give him a lot of attention. When you have conversations with him he talks about himself, and he barely asks you questions about yourself. He wants you to listen to him talk for hours, but he doesn't listen to you talk without cutting you off. He doesn't seem or act interested in anything that you're doing with your life, but he expects you to support his dreams and goals. He won't accompany you to your events, but he'll want you to attend his. The relationship will be very one-sided. He'll want his needs met, but he won't meet your needs. You will feel like the whole relationship is about him, his job, his family and his life. Your family, job, life etc; don't seem important to him at all. Everything is always about him, him and him. When you talk about him he can talk for hours, but when you're talking about yourself he drifts off, changes the subject, seems uninterested or shuts down. Basically, you get the feeling that he just doesn't care about you or your life. In fact, he barely even knows you, but you know a lot about him. You could probably write a book about him, but he won't even be able to write a paragraph about you because he barely knows you. That's because he doesn't try to get to know you, and he really doesn't care to get to know you. Also, he barely apologizes because he thinks he's always right. I mean how can someone so perfect like him be wrong? Even if he were wrong he wouldn't admit that to you because then he would have to admit to being imperfect or wrong, and he has too much pride for that. When he gets mad at you, he lashes out and belittles you to try to bring you down. He gets mad at you when you point out the things that he does wrong because it hurts his ego, and it proves that he isn't as great as he thinks he is. He acts like he's a celebrity, and he wants you to act like you're his biggest fan. Basically, Mr. Narc only cares about himself, and he keeps you around because he loves the attention you give him. Find a guy that wants to hear about your day, and supports you too. It's okay to be your man's cheerleader, but he should also be cheering you on as well. Also, if you are always asking him questions, and he barely asks you questions back it's obvious that he isn't into you. If he were he would help keep the conversation going. Stop being this guy's audience, and go find a guy that is willing to share the stage with you. Know your worth, and kick Mr. Narc out of the spotlight, and off the stage. It's time to close the curtain on him because his show is all about him, and he won't even allow you to be in it.

Mr. Hypocrite

This Mr. Wrong is usually very religious or should I say pretends to be very religious. He is constantly telling everyone including you that they shouldn't be doing certain things because it's against his religion. However, he does things that his religion doesn't approve of as well. In fact, he might do things someone who considers himself religious should never do. Mr. Hypocrite judges' others, but he can't see fault in himself. This Mr. Wrong uses the bible to get women to trust him or believe in him. He's usually a pastor, minister or a well-respected member of a church. He lives a double life. One of his lives is a deeply religious man, and the other one is completely opposite of what he preaches. When you're with a man that is criticizing you and judging you for your actions, but he's doing the same things or worse run. Just because someone claims to be religious it doesn't mean that they are. Throughout history pastors, priest and so called 'men of god' have been involved in scandals that have shocked their congregation and the world. This Mr. Wrong uses the bible to get paid, get women, get people to trust him, and to judge others. It won't take long for you to realize that he's not practicing what he's preaching. However, he will expect you to follow his religion and practice what he preaches. If you don't he'll try to shame you into doing it or threaten to leave you because you're not following his religion.

Mr. Moocher

Believe it or not, some men are gold diggers. They are constantly looking for women to mooch off of, and take care of them. When you're with this guy he will start asking you to buy him things, and he might even try to move in with you really fast. Usually, this guy won't have a job or he'll have a job but he'll keep mentioning things that he wants. He'll complain to you about his financial problems. He'll tell you his phone will be off soon or that he needs money to come to see you. This guy isn't afraid to ask you to pay for dates or buy him his favorite cd. Most guys want to pay for the first date, but this guy wants you to pay for your half or for the whole meal. Some women are okay with paying half of the bill, and that's fine. However, if he's asking you to pay for the whole meal, and you just met him run. Some women spend their whole paycheck on Mr. Moocher, and most of the time he isn't even committed to them. Unless you're in a long-term committed relationship you shouldn't be paying his bills. If he's your friend or friends with benefits you definitely shouldn't be paying his phone bill. If he's living with you, eating your food, and driving your car around town; but he's not in a relationship with you then you have a moocher on your hands. The only reason you should have for paying a man's bills is if you're in a long-term relationship with him, and he lost his job. Or he's a member of your family you're trying to help out. Other than that you're not obligated to finance him or his lifestyle. Only invest your money into people that are investing in you and the relationship that you have with them. Also, the moocher won't look for a job. He will just sleep all day, and relax while you work. An unemployed man that isn't a moocher will be looking for a job, and he won't feel like a real man if he can't find a job to help you out. A moocher doesn't care if you have to take care of him. He doesn't like to work, and he doesn't plan on working.

Mr. Runner

When you meet this guy everything will be great until you have your first problem with him. As soon as he notices a problem he pulls away or leaves because he can't handle problems. He doesn't know how to communicate his feelings or work out problems. So, he tucks his tail in-between his legs and runs. Whenever he's mad at you, he ignores you or vanishes instead of talks to you. When you have an argument with him he leaves the room or walks out on you. After a while, you'll be afraid to voice your opinion because you know he'll get mad and leave you. He uses his walkouts and silent treatments as of way of controlling you and the situation. He's not great with words. So, instead of arguing back and forth with you, he leaves. Plus, when he leaves he no longer has to listen to you, and he has regained control over the situation. Most runners try to let things die down, and then they come back hoping that you'll drop it. When they leave they think the problem will just magically fix itself by the time they get back. When they come back, and you try to have a conversation with them they'll ask you to drop it or ask you why you're still talking about it. The runner doesn't know how to communicate properly so the relationship problems will remain unsolved until you can't take it anymore. Once you can't take it anymore, and you confront him he runs again. Most runners don't commit to you because they want to be able to run at any time. If he doesn't commit to you he can leave you or vanish without having to explain himself to you. However, some do commit but instead of vanishing from your life they vanish for hours, days or weeks without contacting you then they show back up again. Some runners only like the honeymoon stage of the relationship, and when things get rocky they vanish. They want a fairy-tale relationship with no problems or arguments, and they leave women who argue with them. They can't handle the emotions that women have so they run when women start to display these emotions. Never trust a man that runs from his problems because he'll leave you as soon as things get tough. When things are bad you need someone that will stand by your side and help you fight. Not someone that's going to run away like a coward. In order to stay with Mr. Runner, you have to pretend like everything is perfect when it isn't, you can't complain about what he does wrong, and you can't argue too much or he'll pull away from you. Not being able to talk about issues or problems leads to relationship failure because good relationships require good communication. A relationship won't last if a couple can't deal with their problems properly. A runner deals with his relationship problems by running from the problem and replacing the person. Basically, he thinks it's easier to replace you than it is to fix the problem. Runners always take the easy way out. Plus, he thinks that the girl of his dreams won't argue with him and that he'll have a perfect, problem free, relationship with her. He will keep running until he finds this dream girl of his. Which is forever because she doesn't exist. If someone leaves you for a stupid reason they never loved you in the first place, and they're not the type of person you want to settle down with.

Mr. Scammer

This guy is an obvious Mr. Wrong, but some women are new to the Internet, and they don't know he exists. This guy searches for lonely women online, gets to know them, and then he eventually asks them to send him money. Usually, he makes up a sob story or tells them that he can't talk to them or come see them unless they send him money. Some women actually send this Mr. Wrong money not knowing that his profile is completely fake, and he isn't the guy in the picture. If you right click any image online, you will see 'search this image using Google' and it will show you if there are any other profiles online with that image. If that image pops up on other websites investigate the other websites to see if it leads back to the same person. Asks him to do a live chat with you or call you on a local phone number. If he refuses to do a live chat or meet you in person stop talking to him. Also, never send a guy money just for him to come see you or be able to talk to you. Honestly, most real men don't ask women for money. So, if you just met a guy, and he's asking you for money run in the opposite direction. Some scammers ask you to send them money for a phone to call you on or they make up a sob story to get your pity. I've never had a guy asks me for a dime, and I'd never send a dime to a guy that's asking me to pay for his bus trip, plane ticket or gas to come visit me. To each their own, but no matter who you are you should never send large amounts of cash to a total stranger. Most of these scammers are in a totally different country than you are, and they make a living off of scamming lonely people. Once you've been scammed getting your money back will be hard or impossible because they are usually overseas. Never let anyone take advantage of your loneliness. Be smart, and make sure you're talking to a real person.

Chapter 2: SELF-WORTH AND SELF-KNOWLEDGE

Self-Knowledge

In order for you to realize your self-worth, you must love, accept, and know a lot about yourself. A person who doesn't love themselves will think that they're worthless. A person who doesn't accept themselves will be miserable because they hate living in their own skin. A person that feels empty inside or lost doesn't even know who they are so how can they love themselves? Most people that don't know their worth feel empty inside. They wake up every morning and get out of bed just to do their everyday routine. Whenever they look in the mirror they feel distant from their own reflection. Before we go to self-worth we must cover self-knowledge. If you feel empty inside we must dig deep inside you, and unlock the doors that your emotions are hiding behind.

Feeling Empty Inside

Most people tell you that you have to find yourself, but I think you have to create a life for yourself and define yourself. After all, how can you find something that hasn't been created yet? How can you find something if you don't know what you're looking for? How can you find yourself if you think there's nothing to find, and you feel completely empty inside? You might feel like a lost soul trapped inside of someone else's body. You feel as if you just exist, and that you're just floating through life going through the motions. Doing things because it's what you're supposed to do, and doing things because it's what others expect you to do. When you don't know who you are you live your life through other people. You only exist because of the role that you play in their life, but if you stopped playing those roles you wouldn't know what to do with yourself. You only know yourself as a mom, or girlfriend or the nurse or other labels. Without those labels, you don't know who you are. You don't know your real self and just thinking about being alone and not playing those roles makes you feel empty or lonely. If you don't have anyone around you, you feel lost and you don't know what to do with yourself. In order to fix the emptiness you feel, you have to figure out why you're avoiding yourself. Maybe it's because you've been hurt and it hurts too much to face the real you, and all of the pain it feels. Maybe you don't like your life so you live your life through other people to avoid living your own life? Maybe you don't like your life so you pretend to be someone else to avoid the reality of your own life and circumstances? Maybe you gave up on yourself a long time ago, and you don't care about being alive anymore. Maybe, you're just living your life because you have to, and other people need you to. In order to fix the emptiness you have to face yourself, and stop running from yourself. Start living your life instead of just floating through it, and just going through the motions. Stop being a robot, and start being a human that gives themselves permission to express their emotions and feelings. Chances are you have feelings, but you keep them bottled up inside of you or you express them in a negative way. Maybe you feel empty because you've never lived your life for you, and done things that will make you feel happy. Maybe you've only lived your life to please other people, and now that you're alone or getting older you have to finally figure out what you want. Realize that if you feel all of these emotions that you're not empty inside. In order to be empty you have to feel nothing. What you feel is that something is missing, and what's missing is your inability to let yourself feel all of your emotions. All that anger, pain, sadness and misery from the past is hiding inside of you, and you won't feel better until you release all of that misery. Stop holding it in. Just let yourself cry it out. Let yourself feel the anger or the pain. Tell yourself that it's okay to feel hurt, abandoned, neglected, lonely, sad, and mad or whatever else you're feeling. If you've been hurt, you should feel sad because of what happened to you. It's okay to feel the way that you do. Whatever happened to you in your past has caused you to avoid these feelings. Maybe you avoid them because you don't want to feel weak or sad anymore. However, you need to realize that you won't move on until you face your past and stop running from it. Realize that you have survived your past, that you have defeated your enemies, and that you're still standing. Be proud of yourself, and realize that you're not empty inside you're just sad or hurt. If you keep going, and you continue to fight I guarantee you that your life will be better. Queen, you need to realize that you're not empty at all, you have a lot of good things about you, and you're a decent person. How in the world can a nice person such as yourself be empty? If you were empty you wouldn't care about others, and you'd be an emotionless, heartless person. I know you're wondering how I know that you're nice when I don't even know you. Well, a heartless person with no emotions or feelings wouldn't be reading a book to learn how to realize their self-worth. You want to change your life, better yourself, love yourself, and be a little bit happier. So, your eagerness to want to do the above things tells me that you're not that bad of a person. Also, it tells me that you're not empty and that something inside of you is begging you to change your life. That something is your inner thoughts. It's the real you, and it's begging you to give life another chance. It's begging you to love yourself and do something that will make you happier. It's begging you to stop letting people hurt you. It's begging you to go after everything that will make you happy. The fact that you have that voice and those thoughts prove that you're not empty. You're just a sad or hurt person that's been through a lot, and you just want to be happy for once. Your problem is that you ignore your inner voice a lot, and the reason that you ignore it is because you think you can't give it what it wants. It wants you to be happy, but you ignore it because you think you can't make it happy. It wants you to chase your goals or dreams, but you ignore it because you think you can't accomplish them. It wants you to stop letting people use you, but you ignore it because you think you need those people in your life. Basically, that voice is the real you, but you're ignoring yourself and what the real you wants you to do. If you start listening to that voice you'll reconnect with who you are, and what you really want. If you continue to ignore it you'll feel disconnected from yourself, and that disconnection will lead to you feeling empty or like you're a lost soul trapped inside of someone else's body. Also, feeling empty is a sign that you're running from a part of who you are. A part of you might feel sad or hurt, and instead of comforting that part of you, you avoid it, ignore it, or run from it. The reason you ignore it is because that part of you is in pain, and you hate feeling all of the pain it feels. You're hoping that ignoring the pain, and pretending like it doesn't exist will make it go away. Well, until that part of you is accepted by you, and you accept the pain it feels you won't move on. Tell that part of you that it's okay to feel hurt, that it has survived the past, that it's strong, and that you won't ignore how it feels anymore. Tell that part of you that it's okay to cry and that it's okay to be sad. Start comforting that part of you, and telling it that everything will be okay. A person that feels empty inside isn't empty they're just ignoring their inner thoughts, trying to block out unwanted memories, and trying to force the part of them that feels pain to move on in the wrong way.

For example; Tasha's inner voice is telling her that she should move on, and leave a man that isn't treating her right. However, she ignores that voice and stays in a bad relationship. Also, Tasha was physically abused by an ex, but instead of talking to someone about the pain she went through; she tries to block it out of her memory. Instead of helping or comforting the part of herself that feels pain, she tells it to move on, and get over it... However, Tasha can't move on because that part of her is in too much pain to move on, but Tasha pretends like she's okay instead of acknowledging her true feelings. Then

Tasha claims that she's empty inside, but in reality, she's just ignoring herself, her thoughts, and her feelings.

You're ignoring yourself because you hear those thoughts, you feel those feelings, and you remember your past, but you're blocking them out instead of facing them. Then you claim to be empty, but the truth is that you're ignoring who you are.

Starting today, I want you to stop ignoring your inner voice. When that inner voice tells you that it's hurting and that you should move on; listen to it. Also, I want you to stop pretending like your past didn't happen to you. It happened to you, but you were strong enough to survive it. Stop running from your past, and trying to block out unwanted memories. To move on you must accept that your past is a part of your life story. It's a miserable part of your life story, but it's still a part of it. Stop holding back your emotions. Stop telling yourself that crying means that you're weak and that you have to be strong 24/7. Stop trying to force yourself to move on, and start helping yourself to move on. You help yourself to move on by comforting yourself, talking to a counselor, supporting yourself, being there for yourself, and allowing yourself to feel how you really feel. Would you tell a hurt person to shut up and move on or would you comfort them, and try to help them to move on? You would comfort them, be there for them, let them cry on your shoulders, and try to help them move on. Well, if you're hurt you should be doing the same thing for yourself because that's the only way that you're going to move on. Telling yourself to forget about it or to shut up and move on doesn't work. If you do that, you'll be a person that is pretending to be happy when you're really just miserable. Your "I'm fine" and "I'm okay" answers can fool everyone else, but it won't fool you. If you know you're not "okay" or "fine" admit it, and stop denying your true feelings. Being strong doesn't mean that you can't cry, feel hurt or feel down, it means that you don't give up even though you feel like giving up. It means that you still get out of bed every morning even though things in your life aren't perfect. It means that you're still standing even though you've been hurt, abused, played, disrespected or neglected. It's okay to have bad days. In fact, bad days, bad weeks and even a bad year are normal so don't be so hard on yourself.

Realize that your inner thoughts, your emotions, your fears, your strengths, your weaknesses, your desires, your dreams, your wants, your past, and your needs are all parts of you, and if you listen to or acknowledge these parts of you, you'll no longer feel empty.

Reconnect with yourself activity

Read the questions below out loud to yourself. After you read the following questions out loud to yourself give your thoughts time to respond to them truthfully.

1. **Hey me, how are you really feeling today?**

2. **Hey me, what do you want me to do with my life?**

3. Hey me, do you want me to be happy or miserable?

4. Hey me, do you want me to stay with people that abuse me, use me or walk all over me?

5. Hey me, what are some things that you're good at?

Every day ask yourself how you're doing, and how you really feel about yourself and your life. Tell yourself the truth, acknowledge your feelings, and stop ignoring yourself.

I'm hoping that I can help you on your journey to self-love, and realizing your self-worth. Think of me as your online friend. A friend that's been down some of the same dark roads that you've been on. A friend that is willing to show you the way out of the darkness, and into the light. I'm living proof that happiness can come after misery. There's a lot of love in you. You're not empty, you're full of niceness, but you just haven't met people that have appreciated your kindness.

SELF-WORTH

An important part of dating is knowing your self-worth. Not knowing your worth leads to poor dating choices, and dating the wrong type of people. A person that doesn't know their self-worth puts up with disrespect, abuse, being used, being walked over, and all kinds of things a person shouldn't put up with. A lot of people these days don't know their worth. They say they know their worth, but their actions prove that they don't. Once a person knows their worth they don't put up with disrespect because they know they deserve to be treated better than that. A person that knows their worth loves themselves too much to let someone walk all over them or treat them wrong. Since knowing your self-worth is a part of not getting played we will go over that first.

"You have flaws, you've made mistakes, and you're far from perfect, but you still deserve to be treated like a Queen."

Realize that your self-worth isn't determined by how you look; it's determined by how much you think your worth.

Example: Mandy and Jill are identical twins. They look exactly alike. Mandy hates how she looks because she has freckles, and she has low self-esteem because of it. Jill loves her freckles because she thinks it makes her unique. Jill has accepted that her freckles are a part of who she is, and she has high self-esteem.

In the above scenario both girls look exactly the same, so their worth wasn't determined by their looks, it was determined by what they thought of themselves.

Realize that your worth isn't determined by

1. How you look
2. How much money you have
3. How successful you are
4. How many friends you have
5. Who loves you, and who doesn't
6. Whether you're popular or not

Yet most people base their self-worth on the above things. Basing your self-worth on things that can change at any time leads to your sense of self-worth lowering at any given moment. It leads to you basing your self-worth on things that you have no control over or things you can't change. Basing your self-worth on things you can't change leads to you thinking that you're worthless and that you'll always be worthless because of that problem that you can't change. If you think that you have to be rich in order to be worth something, what happens if you lose all of your money? If you lost all of your money you would think that you were worthless because to you having money equals worth. If you think your worth is determined by how beautiful you are, you will think that you're worthless because of your flaws or other physical things. You would also think that women who are prettier than you are worth more than you, and that you are beneath them. If you base your self-worth on not being loved by someone, you will feel worthless every time someone rejects you. Your self-worth should never be based on things like money, looks, success or not being loved by someone. That leads to an up and down sense of self-worth. One minute you'll think you're worth a lot because you reached one of your goals, and the next minute you'll think you're worthless because you failed a test. **You should base your self-worth on who you are as a person, and how you want to be treated.** If you're a nice person, know your worth and realize that you deserve to be treated nicely. Should a nice person be treated badly? Nope. They deserve to be treated with the same respect and love that they show others.

Answer the following questions

1. Does your self-worth go up and down?

2. Does your self-worth depend on what others think of you?

3. Do you base your self-worth on how you look?

4. Do you base your self-worth on how much money you have?

5. Do you base your self-worth on how successful you are?

6. Do you base your self-worth on what the person you love thinks of you?

7. Does being rejected make you feel worthless?

8. Does being rejected make you feel like you're not good enough?

9. Do you think that other women are worth more than you are just because they look better, or dress nicer, or are richer than you are?

If you answered 'yes' to one of the above, you are basing your self-worth on the wrong things. You're letting things you can't control, things that aren't important, and people that don't belong in your life control your self-worth.

Toya thinks the models in her magazine are worth more than she is simply because they are considered more beautiful than she is. She thinks the models deserve a man that will treat them right, but she thinks she will never find a man that will treat her like a Queen because of the way she looks. Toya is constantly comparing herself to other women, and thinking that they are better than her and worth more than her.

In the above scenario, Toya is basing her self-worth on how she looks. Basing your self-worth on looks leads to you putting others above you just because you think they look better than you.

1. If you think they're worth more than you just because of their looks, wealth or popularity you're basing your self-worth on the wrong things
2. Just because someone is smarter, prettier, wealthier or more popular than you are, it doesn't mean that their life is worth more than yours

Starting today I want you to base your self-worth on who you really are inside, and how you want to be treated; NOT by how you look

Realize that you might not be the prettiest, smartest, most popular or richest girl on the planet, but you still deserve to be treated right.

Jill has 2 dogs. One of her dogs has a broken leg, and the other one doesn't.

- *Which dog should she be mean to?*

- *Which dog should she hate?*

- *Which dog doesn't deserve to be loved?*

If you answered 'none' that is the correct answer. In the above, you agreed that both dogs deserved to be loved even though one has a flaw, and one doesn't. Just because one dog has a flaw, and the other one doesn't it doesn't mean that one is worthless. Just because you have more flaws than someone else it doesn't mean that you're worthless or that you deserve to be treated like crap. If you think Jill should be nice to the dog with the flaw, then you should think that people should be nice to you too. Isn't your life just as important as a dog's life? If you think you're worthless because of your flaws, and that you're not good enough to be loved. You might as well say that the dog with the broken leg is worthless because of his flaws that he should be treated wrong and that Jill shouldn't love him. It's kind of sad when you think about it, but when you don't love yourself or know your worth you don't care about yourself. You might care about the dog or other people, but you don't care that much about yourself. You don't show yourself the same LOVE that you show others. Also, just because the other dog doesn't have a more noticeable flaw it doesn't mean that it's flawless. Everyone has flaws it's just that some people's flaws are more noticeable than others. The above example proves that everyone should be treated the same regardless of their flaws. Never think that someone else should be treated better than you just because your flaws are more noticeable than theirs are. Always apply your beliefs of what's right and wrong to your own life too.

If your best friend told you that they were worthless because they couldn't find a job you would tell them that they weren't worthless. Do you know why you would tell them that? You would tell them that because when you look at your friends you don't judge them because of their flaws, you don't hate them because of their failures, and you don't care if they aren't successful. You just love your friends for who they are, flaws and all. When you look at a friend you see a person that deserves everything they want in life, a person that deserves to be happy, and a person that deserves to be treated right.

However, when you call yourself worthless you don't look past your own flaws or failures. Instead, you focus on them, point them out, highlight them, and you constantly put yourself down because of them. When you look at yourself you don't see a person that deserves to be loved for who they are flaws and all. You see a person that deserves to be treated like their nothing because you think you're nothing. Whenever you think you're not good enough you don't cheer yourself up like you do your friends; you just let yourself feel that way. When a friend is feeling down you try to pick them up, but when you're feeling down you kick yourself while you're down. A person that knows their worth is their own personal cheerleader. When you fail tell yourself that it's okay and that you can try again. When you fall tell yourself that it's okay and that things will get better or that you'll find a way to get back up. When you make a mistake tell yourself that's it's okay, and that everyone makes mistakes. When you get rejected tell yourself that they weren't meant to be with you and that you'll find someone else one day. Tell yourself the same thing that you would tell a friend. When a friend feels worthless you tell them all the good things about themselves, you hug them and show them love. When you feel worthless or down start doing that for yourself. Be your own best friend. Every time a negative thought about yourself pops into your head replace it with a positive thought about yourself. Whenever your friends say something negative about themselves you tell them something positive to cheer them up, and you try to boost their self-confidence. Start doing that for yourself. Once you start focusing on the positive things about yourself, and you stop tearing yourself apart your life will be better. Your life will be better because you'll realize that there are plenty of good things about you and that life can be great. Life can be great you're just so busy focusing on the negative things in life that you can't enjoy the positive things in life. Look around at your life, and be thankful for what you do have. Be proud of yourself for surviving your past. Be proud of yourself for the things you have accomplished. Maybe you're a good mom, a good student, a nice person who helps everyone or maybe you're really good at something. If you spend your time focusing on and expanding the positive things about yourself, your life will get better, and you'll be happier.

A woman that knows her worth says **"I know I'm not perfect, I know I've made mistakes, I know I've been rejected, I know that I'm not as successful as I want to be, and I know that I have flaws, but I'm still a GREAT PERSON. Those things are a part of my life story, but they don't define who I am as a person. Even though I'm not perfect I still want to be loved, and I still want to be treated like a Queen. I deserve to be treated nicely because I'm a nice person."**

WHAT IS A FLAW?

Most people know what a flaw is. However, let's dig a little deeper beyond the obvious. Starting today, I want you to realize that society labels anything that isn't perfect as a flaw, and when you think about it, it's kind of ridiculous. It's ridiculous because when you label everything that isn't perfect as flawed; you're calling everyone on the planet flawed, and you're calling the way they were born flawed. Basically, as soon as you're born you're labeled flawed because you're not perfect. How a person was made, born or created is normal for them. Other people might see it as abnormal or a flaw, but it's completely normal for the person that was born that way. Realize that how you were born isn't a flaw it's just how you were created. Society just calls it a flaw because it doesn't fit society's definition of normal or perfect. Most people hate their so called flaws because society judges them for it. Every magazine is filled with comments like; look who gained weight, look who had plastic surgery, look who's gotten too thin, look who's on a diet, look at what she was wearing or who wore this dress the best. Our society is obsessed with looks, and it puts every woman under a microscope and tears her apart. Every woman is judged by her appearance, and it leads to women constantly being obsessed with their looks.

Also, it leads to women basing their self-worth on their appearance. Magazines even have a contest that lists the hottest women on the planet. Sadly, society is starting to judge a woman's worth on how she looks instead of who she is as a person. Most modern day women spend a lot of money just so they can compete in society's 'who looks the best' competitions. From now on, try not to get sucked into society's competitions; competitions where they rip women apart and judge a woman's worth by her looks. Realize that you don't have to compete in the 'who looks better competitions'. Just live your life, and focus on other things that you have to offer. Play by your rule's not the rules' that society wants you to play by.

"Personally, I want to be known for what I have done for the world, not for how 'sexy' I looked in a dress."

Realize that you're a great person. Start focusing on the good things about yourself, and stop focusing on the negative things about yourself. Even though your family and friends have flaws and problems you still love them because you focus on the good stuff about them. You're a great person that deserves to be loved for who you are flaws and all, but finding love starts with loving yourself Lets go to step 1 on your journey to realizing your worth.

STEP 1: DON'T REJECT YOURSELF

When someone rejects you it hurts because you love them, and you want them to love you back. But what happens when the person rejecting you is the person in your mirror? Every time you look in your mirror you reject parts of yourself because you're unhappy with your looks, your flaws or your life. Realize that rejecting yourself lowers your self-esteem, self-worth, self-respect, and self-confidence. When you reject yourself you're telling yourself that you're not good enough to be loved'. You're looking in your mirror, and you're telling yourself that you can't love yourself because of your flaws or problems. You're telling yourself that you're not good enough to be loved by you. Then you go out into the world looking for someone to love you flaws and all when you don't even love yourself flaws and all. Then you tell everyone that you love yourself and that you know your worth but in reality, you're your number 1 hater or enemy. Starting today I want you to accept yourself for who you are flaws and all. The person in your mirror doesn't want you to reject them anymore. The person in your mirror wants you to love them for who they are flaws and all. What do they have to do in order for you to love them?

1. Are you looking at the person in your mirror, and telling them that you don't love them?

2. Are you telling them that they're not good enough to be loved?

3. Are you telling them that they're worthless or that you hate them because of their flaws?

4. Have you stopped taking care of the person in your mirror?

If so, it's time for you to stop treating yourself wrong. You should never treat yourself that way. The person in your mirror hasn't done anything to deserve to be treated like that.

Activity 1

Answer the following questions

1. When you look into your mirror what do you dislike about yourself? Write down the things you dislike about yourself.

2. Look at the things you've written down, and next to each one write down whether it can be changed or not.

3. For the things that can be changed, make a plan for changing it. For the things that can't be changed, you have to accept it.

For the things that can't be changed.

1. Are you really going to hate yourself because of those things?

2. Is that how you're going to treat yourself?

3. Is that being fair to yourself?

4. Is that how you treat someone that you're supposed to love?

When you love someone you don't hate them because of their flaws. You don't reject them, and you don't put them down because of their flaws. Basically, you're telling yourself that you can't love yourself because of your flaws or problems. Stop treating yourself like that.

Activity 2

1. Go look in your mirror, and tell the person in your mirror that you're done treating them like crap. Tell them that you're going to love them for who they are flaws and all. It's not their fault that they have those flaws. So, why are you blaming them for it? Why are you putting them down for things they can't change?

2. Apologize to the person in your mirror because they don't deserve to be treated like that. Before you go to step 2 look in your mirror and apologize to yourself for treating yourself wrong. Tell the person in your mirror that you're going to start showing them some love.

3. Read the following out loud. **"Dear self" I'm sorry for how I've been treating myself. I know I haven't loved myself the way I'm supposed to love myself, but starting right now that's going to change. In the past, I have put myself down, but starting right now I'm going to build myself up. In the past, I rejected myself because of how I look, but starting now I will accept myself for who I am, flaws and all. In the past I hated myself, but starting right now I'm going to show myself some love. Changing the way I treat myself will take some time, but I promise myself that I will treat myself better than I did before. It's my job to love myself, but I haven't done my job, but starting right now I will do my job. I know I have flaws that I can't change, but I will love myself anyway. I deserved to be loved for who I am, and I'm good enough to be loved by me. Dear person in my mirror: I love you, and I hope you can forgive me, and accept my apology. You don't deserve to be treated wrong, and I promise to treat you better. Sincerely, me.**

STEP 2: SHOW YOURSELF SOME LOVE

At one point in my life, I realized that I was focusing on the negative things about myself more than the positive things. However, once I begin to focus on the positive things more than the negative things my life became better. When you focus on negative things your life seems worse than what it is. You're constantly thinking about what's wrong with you and your life, then you're always miserable because of all that negative energy. Starting today I need you to shower yourself with positivity instead of negativity. I know you have flaws, but what are some good things about you?

Activity 3.

1. Write down 10 things you like about yourself

2. Write down 5 things you're good at

3. Go look in your mirror right now and give yourself 5 compliments

My five compliments

1. _____

2. _____

3. _____

4. _____

5. _____

See there's plenty of good things about you, and if you focus on the good things, and find a way to use your talents your life will change for the better. Starting today every time you bash yourself you have to give yourself 2 compliments. The next time you make fun of yourself or put yourself down you have to apologize to yourself and give yourself two compliments. When someone else hurts you they have to apologize to you for it, and after they apologize you hope they won't hurt you again. Starting today you have to apologize to yourself for hurting yourself because it will remind you that you are wrong for treating yourself like that. This will help you to treat yourself better and show yourself more love.

STEP 3: IS TO BE WILLING TO MAKE YOURSELF HAPPY.

A lot of people with low self-worth tend to care about others more than they care about themselves. They will go out of their way to make someone else happy, but they barely do anything to make themselves happy. They break their back for everyone they love, but when it comes to themselves they give up. Starting today I want you to be willing to go out of your way for yourself and be willing to break your back so that you can be happy. All of those things you did for the wrong person should have been done for yourself. In order to be happy you have to find out what's making you unhappy and do something about it.

Activity 4.

1. Write down 5 things besides flaws or things that you can't change that you're unhappy about.
   These are things that you CAN change with hard work and determination.

   Since these are things that you can CHANGE, how will you change them

   I'm unhappy because _____

   How will you fix the above issue? _____

   I'm unhappy because _____

   How will you fix the above issue? _____

   I'm unhappy because _____

How will you fix the above issue? _____

I'm unhappy because _____

How will you fix the above issue? _____

I'm unhappy because _____

How will you fix the above issue? _____

2. Write down why you haven't done anything to fix those things

3. When will you take the first step to fix them?

Starting today I want you to stop making excuses for why you're not doing everything you can to make yourself happy. You're breaking your back to make other people happy, and you're not doing anything for yourself. Then you wonder why you're miserable and unhappy? Instead of doing everything you can for Mr. Wrong start doing things for yourself. All of that time you wasted TRYING to make him happy could have been spent on you and your happiness.

Activity 5.

Read this out loud to yourself. **"Dear self: I've spent so much time trying to make other people happy that I've forgotten about my own happiness. I break my back for them, and I don't even break a sweat for myself. Starting today, I'm going to do whatever it takes to make myself happy because I deserve to be happy too. I'm going to chase my goals and dreams and break my back for myself like I do everyone else. Dear person in my mirror: I love you, and I want you to know that I will do whatever it takes to make myself happy. If you want me to chase my goals, I'll do it. If you want me to chase my dreams I'll do it. If you want me to fight for what you want, I'll do it. My happiness matters to me, and I promise I won't forget about my happiness again. Sincerely me.**

STEP 4: REALIZE THAT YOU'RE A QUEEN

Yes, girl. Realize that you're the queen of your life. You wear the crown, and whoever doesn't like you for you can get out of your life. Yes, girl. You rule your life, and whoever doesn't like the way you live your life can get out of your life. You are a Queen, and you deserve to be with A King. A King knows how to treat a Queen like you, and you deserve to be treated well. Yes, girl. There is not another girl like you on this planet, you are the original, and you are unique. Wear your crown proudly. Hold your head up high, and walk like a Queen.

If they don't like you, the way you live your life or the way you look they can get out of your life because you don't need people like that in your life. You're the Queen of your life, and you decide who stays and who goes. You decide what you will, and what you won't put up with. Haters and enemies aren't welcome in your life because you only want positive people in your kingdom, positive people living in your house, and positive energy around you. Yes girl, never forget that you are a Queen, and you rule your life.

STEP 5: IS TO CARE ABOUT YOURSELF

People claim to care about themselves, but their actions prove they don't. When you care about someone you love them and protect them. How is staying with someone that abuses you, cheats on you, uses you or walks over you protecting yourself? If you're not protecting yourself, you're not caring about yourself. I care about you, but I'm going to let people hurt you? Does that make sense? Nope. If you care about yourself prove it by walking away from people that constantly disrespect you. Whenever you want to know if someone is treating you right or not Ask yourself this " Would I want someone I CARE about to be treated like this? If the answer is 'no' then you aren't getting treated right, and if you cared about yourself like you claim you wouldn't want yourself to be treated like that either. Why is it okay for them to hurt you, but it's not okay for them to hurt your mother, your sister or your friends? It's because you care about your mother, your sister or your friends, but you don't care about yourself. Starting today I need you to care about yourself, and what people do to you. Stop letting people treat you like that. Start protecting yourself like you protect your family and friends. If someone hurts your family or friends you get MAD at the person that hurt them, and you try to protect your friend or family member. However, if someone hurts you, you hold onto them, and let them hurt you over and over again. Why is okay for people to hurt you, but it's not okay for them to hurt your family or friends. It's because you love your friends and family with all your heart, but you don't love yourself with all of your heart. Start showing yourself some freaking love. Get mad when people hurt you, and protect yourself from those who hurt you over and over again. Realize that you're a Queen. Yes, girl, you're a queen and you don't deserve to treated that way.

Activity 6.

Read this out loud to yourself **"Dear self, I've realized that I haven't had my own back. I have everyone else's back, and I look out for them, but I don't do the same for myself. I let people do things to me that I know isn't right. I let people hurt me over and over again. It's my job to protect myself, but I haven't been doing my job. Starting today, I'm going to have my own back. If anyone hurts me they have to answer to me. When someone hurts my friends or family I get mad at them, but when someone hurts me I hold onto them or let them get away with it. I realize that I haven't been caring about myself as much as I should. I apologize for not having my own back, but from now on I will. Please accept my apology. Sincerely me.**

STEP 6: STOP PUTTING UP WITH DISRESPECT

When you don't know your worth you put up with disrespect. You think you're not worthy of love or you don't know what real love is. Maybe you've only been with men who've treated you wrong so being treated wrong is normal to you. Realize that constant disrespect isn't love. Be honest with yourself. In your life, you've put up with things that you knew weren't right. You're a Queen and you knew he wasn't' treating you right, but you stayed anyway. You let men use you and walk all over you and you knew you deserved better. You knew it wasn't love, you knew they didn't love you, but you stayed. You stayed because you thought you could change them or make them love you. You put up with their disrespect because you didn't want to be alone, and you wanted a fairy tale ending. You might have had sex with a man that you knew didn't care about you. You might have stayed with a man that cheated on you over and over again even though you knew he was putting your health at risk.

Activity 7

1. Write down 5 things that you've put up with from men that you know weren't right

2. Next to those 5 things write down why you put with those things.

- Was it because you thought you could change them?

- Was it because you thought it would make them love you?

- Was it because you thought you had to prove yourself to them?

- Was it because you thought they loved you?

Read this out loud to yourself **"Dear self: I've let men do things to me that I knew wasn't right. I knew it wasn't right, but I put up with it anyway. I was hoping that I could change them and make them love me, but they never did. I'm sorry for letting men use me for sex, for letting men walk all over me, and for letting men disrespect me over and over again. The sad thing is that I knew they didn't love me, but I made myself stay anyway. I should have had my own back, but I didn't. I apologize for making myself put up with those things. I didn't deserve it, and from now on I won't let men use me, walk all over me, and disrespect me over and over again. I apologize for allowing men to use me, walk all over me, and treat me wrong. Please accept my apology. Sincerely me.**

STEP 7: IS TO TAKE CARE OF YOURSELF

When a person doesn't know their worth or love themselves they don't take care of themselves they would they should. Even though you have flaws and you're not perfect you should still take care of yourself. Girl, you have to work with what you've got. Fix your hair, do your nails, put on some perfume, and dress as best as you can. When you take care of yourself and look as best as you can it boost your confidence. Also, it attracts more men because men like women who take care of themselves. No matter what size you are work with what you've got. No matter what flaws you have work with what you've got. There are celebrities of all sizes and shapes who worked with what they had and made it to the top. Never use your flaws as an excuse for not being able to live your life or reach your goals and dreams. If you live your life as if you don't have that flaw your life will be better. Find a celebrity with your body type, and use them as inspiration and motivation to better your own life. If they can succeed so can you. NO EXCUSES.

Jane hates her flaws so she doesn't take care of herself anymore. She wears clothes with stains, she doesn't do anything to her hair, and she doesn't do anything to make herself look presentable.

Even though Jane has flaws that isn't a good excuse to let the rest of herself go. If she takes care of the rest of herself, it will boost her confidence. She should highlight her best features, and work with what she's got. Your worth isn't determined by what you wear, but wearing stained clothes, and having messy hair is a sign that you're not taking care of yourself. If you can't afford stain free clothes there are shops and thrift stores that have low priced clothing. Also, there are charities that give away clothing for free. So, unless you're homeless there isn't a good excuse for not brushing your hair, and walking around with stained clothing.

Mandy dislikes her stomach, but she loves her legs. So, she works with what she's got by wearing outfits that show off her legs. She isn't letting her whole self-go just because of that one flaw.

You have to work with what you've got. Working with what you've got and highlighting your best features will boost your confidence. Letting yourself go will lower your self-confidence.

If you've ever watched a make-over show, you know that the women look and feel better when they just spend a few hours taking care of their appearance. Spend a few hours pampering yourself, and taking care of yourself and you'll look and feel better. Have a 'me' day where you get your nails done or a massage. Spoil yourself sometimes, and treat yourself like a Queen. Some women want a man to treat them like a Queen, but they don't even treat themselves like a Queen. Love yourself before you look for someone else to love you.

Activity 8

Write down 3 things you can do to improve yourself. Like brushing your teeth more, ironing your clothes, a new hairstyle, a new wardrobe, taking care of your hygiene, smelling better, wearing clothes that fit you better, waxing facial hair, eating healthier foods etc. Work with what you've got, and improve on the things you know can be better.

Activity 9

Read this out loud to yourself: **Dear self: Starting today I'm going to work with what I've got. I'm not the hottest girl on the planet, but that doesn't mean that I shouldn't take care of myself. I apologize for not taking care of myself like I should. I'm a Queen and I should be pampering, and treating myself like one. Starting today I'm going to take care of myself and make sure that I look as best as I can. If I want a man to treat me like a Queen, I need to treat myself like a Queen too. Sincerely me.**

1. Sally hates her lips, but she loves her eyes so she works with what she's got by adding makeup to her eyes. Highlighting her best feature has gotten her tons of compliments.
2. Mary hates her stomach, but she loves her legs. So, she works with what she's got by wearing outfits that show off her legs.

Yes girl, work with what you've got and improve the things you know you can improve.

What are some ways that you can improve yourself by working with What You've Got?

STEP 8: DON'T HATE ON OTHER WOMEN

Don't hate on another woman just because she has something you don't have. Just focus on how you can make your own life better. Focusing on how great her life is isn't going to change your life. Her life is great because she is chasing her goals, and working with what she's got. If you want your life to be great you have to do the same. Once you change your life, and you're happy with it, you won't be jealous of others anymore. You're jealous because you're unhappy with your own life. Most women have been through some of the same hurtful things in life, and the last thing a hurt woman needs is another hurt woman bringing her down because of jealousy, ignorance or insecurities

Activity 10

Answer the following questions.

1. What are you jealous of others about? Write down 3 things.

2. What can you do to fix your own life so you can be happy with it? Write down 3 things.

3. When are you going to fix your life so you can be happy with it? Start making small changes in your life today.

Read this out loud to yourself **"Dear self: I know I'm jealous of her because she has something that I don't, but I need to realize that she isn't me and that there are good things about me too. If I focus on the good things about myself and fix my own life, I'll be happy too. Starting today I'm going to make sure that I focus on my life instead of everyone else's. Also, I'm going to fix the things in my life that I** can change, and I'm going to stop letting the things I can't change hold me back in life. I've been so focused on the things I can't fix in my life that I haven't fixed the things I can fix in my life. I apologize for spending so much time focusing on others instead of focusing on myself, my life and my happiness. Starting today I promise to spend more of my time focusing on myself, my life and my own happiness. Sincerely me."

STEP 9: STAND UP FOR YOURSELF

There are people in this world that will walk all over you, step on you and take advantage of you if you let them. That's why you have to stand up for yourself. If someone does something to you that you dislike tell them immediately. Let them know that you don't put up with disrespect. If you don't they will think it's okay to treat you that way, and they will keep doing it. Disrespect starts off with small things then it leads to bigger and badder things. So, put your foot down at the first sign of it. If a man tells you he is going to pick you up and he never shows up. Tell him that the next time he does it you won't be seeing him again. If someone hangs up on you tell them that you don't like people hanging up on you, and you want them to tell you goodbye instead of just hanging up on you. Let people know what you don't put up with, and they'll know they can't walk all over you. Being afraid to speak your mind and stand up for yourself will get you walked over, and constantly disrespected. You are a Queen and people should show you the same respect that you show them. If you're treating them right they should be treating you right, no excuses.

Activity 11

Read this out loud to yourself.: **"Dear Self: I know I haven't stood up for myself as much as I should. From now on when someone is rude or disrespectful to me, I will stand up for myself, and let them know that I don't put up with disrespect. I will no longer let people think it's OKAY to treat me like crap. I will speak up for myself, defend myself, and stand up for myself no matter what. I apologize for letting people get away with stuff before, but I promise they won't get away with disrespecting me anymore. Anyone that disrespects me, and acts like they don't care about me will be cut out of my life. I'm a Queen, and I don't deserve to be treated wrong. Sincerely me."**

STEP 10: GIVING YOU ALL TO MEN YOU KNOW DON'T LOVE YOU

Your instincts and your soul are telling you that he is Mr. Wrong. Your instincts are telling you that he doesn't love you. Yet you continue to give this man everything you've got. A man shouldn't be allowed to sleep with you if he doesn't care about you. A man that constantly disrespects you doesn't deserve all of your love and affection. A man that beats you walks all over, uses you, and doesn't love you doesn't deserve a nice girl like you. If you're a nice girl you should with someone that will treat you right. You should never be someone's booty call, friend with benefits, side chick because that's saying that all you're good for is sex. Is Sex all you think you're good for? Think about how much of yourself you're giving to a man that doesn't love you. All of that love is going to the wrong man. How much love is he showing you? If he's isn't showing you any love you need to let go of him. I'm not talking about fake love I'm talking about real love.

- **Is he committed to you?** _____ If not, why are you giving this man all you've got? Why are you playing wife to a man that isn't claiming you? He doesn't even want to be with you, but you're giving this man sex and everything else he wants. Now, what is this man doing for you besides waste your time? If nothing you need to move on. Find a man that wants to claim you as his Queen. Yes girl, you're a Queen and you need a King, not a Mr. Wrong that is wasting your time. Find a man that wants all of you not parts of you. You're holding onto a man that is saying I want your sex, and everything else you've got, but I don't want you. Is that all you think your worth?
- **Is he being faithful to you?** _____If not, why are you holding onto a man that wants you and every other woman that is willing to open her legs for him? He's putting your health at risk, and he's disrespecting you. He's saying that you're not good enough for him, and he needs other women. Realize that you're good enough but you're just settling for less. Basically, he says he's committed to you, but he's acting like he's still single. Is this the type of man you want to marry and have a family with? Would you want your mom or daughter to be with a man that cheats on them? Nope! Because you know they deserve better. So, what about you? Don't you think you deserve better?

Activity 12

Read this out loud to yourself: "**Dear self. I'm sorry for letting men I know don't love me use me for sex. I thought they would love me one day. I thought everything I was doing for them, and with them would lead to something more. I thought I could make them love me. I'm sorry for staying with men that acted like I wasn't good enough for them. I thought I could change their mind about me, and make them love me the way I should be loved. From now on I will leave a man who acts like I'm not good enough for him. I'm a Queen, and I need a King that will be with me and only me. I'm a Queen and I deserve a man that wants to commit to me and be faithful to me. I'm a Queen and I deserve to be someone's wife, not someone's booty call, side chick or friend with benefits. From now on I won't settle for less than I'm worth. If a man doesn't want the whole package he can walk away with nothing. Sincerely me.**"

STEP 11: GIVING UP ON YOURSELF

Look around at your life, and where you're at right now. If you're not happy with where you're at in life you need to make changes NOW. When you're unhappy with your life that lowers your self-confidence and it leads to you lowering your self-worth. If you feel like a failure, you'll settle for people that treat you like you're a failure. You'll think that you're a loser and that you deserve to be with a loser. Starting today you need to get your life back on the right track. Once you're back on the right track your confidence will improve because you'll be happier and proud of yourself for making positive changes. Then you'll believe in yourself and raise your self-worth.

Activity 13.

Answer the following questions

1. Are you giving life all you've got?

2. Are you fighting for what you want in life?

3. Have you given up on your goals and dreams?

4. Have you thought about ending your life?

5. Have you fallen and you think you can't get back up?

If you answered yes to one or more of the above questions you've given up, and a person that gives up doesn't know their worth. If you knew your worth you would be focusing on your strengths and finding a way to use your talents. A negative person thinks about how bad their life is, and a positive person thinks about how they can make their life better. Start looking at life in a positive way. Bad things will happen to you, but you can't let those things ruining your whole life. Somehow, some way you always have to find a way to move on.

How can you make your life better?

1. Write down 1 thing you can do today to make your life a little better

2. Write down 5 things you can do that will make you proud of yourself

3. Write down 3 things you can do by next year that will change your life and make you happier.

If you started it today, you can get it done by next year. You just have to fight and fight and fight until it changes. Yes girl, you're a Queen and you can do it. You just have to believe in yourself. A Queen doesn't give up. She just keeps fighting until she finds a way for something to change. In my book 29 Steps to Getting Your Life Back on the Right Track" I go over this in more detail.

Activity 14

Read this out loud to yourself. **"Dear Self: I haven't given life or myself my all. However, starting today I'm going to show myself and the world what I can do. I'm going to fight until my life changes. I'm not a quitter, I'm a fighter, and it's not over until I say it's over. I apologize for wasting so much time and giving up on myself, but I promise that I will make it up to myself. I'm going to do things that will make me proud of myself, and one day I'm going to make my dreams come true. Starting today I'm living my life for me. No more excuses, no more broken promises to myself. This time I'm giving life my all. I love myself and I WILL never give up on myself again. Sincerely me."**

STEP 12: REALIZE HOW STRONG YOU ARE

Some women have been through a lot in life. Things that haunt them and make them miserable

1. Heartbreak

2. Rape

3. Molestation

4. Domestic Violence

5. Childhood Abuse

However, you have to realize that you have survived. Even though it was one of the worst things that have ever happened to you, you have survived it. Yes, girl, you're a Queen and you are very strong. Your enemies tried to knock you down, but you're still standing. Even though you feel like giving up on life you still keep going. Your strength keeps you going... You defeated your past, and now it's time for you to focus on the present so you can have a better future. They tried to bring you down, but you got back up, and you still keep getting out of bed every morning to fight another day. Your strength is amazing, and if you use that strength to chase after the things you want in life you'll be surprised at how far you can go. Realize that you're still standing for a reason. They shouldn't have hurt you. You didn't deserve it; they were wrong for what they did. God has a plan for you, and you have been given another chance to live your life. In my book "22 Steps to Letting Go of Past Hurts" I go over this in more detail. Always remember that you're a Queen and it's not over until you say it's over. Sure you'll fall, but you'll just get back up. Sure you'll fail, but you'll just try again. Sure you'll get hurt, but you won't let it stop you from chasing happiness. If you were strong enough to get through your past you're strong enough to get through the things you're going through now.

STEP 13: DETERMINE YOUR WORTH

How do you want to be treated?

ACTIVITY 15

Read the following sentences out loud to yourself, and pick the type of relationship that you WANT.

1. I want to be treated like a Queen. I want to be loved by someone that loves me back and treats me like a Queen. I want to be with someone that wants to be with me.
2. I want to be treated like I'm nothing. I want to be with someone that treats me like crap and walks all over me.
3. I want to be used. I only want to be with men that use me for sex. I want to give my all to men who don't love me. I want men to come around when they want sex, and then leave me.
4. I want to be disrespected. I want to be with a man that I have to share with other women. A man that cheats on me, and puts my health at risk.
5. I want to be abused. I want to be with a man that hits me or verbally abuses me. I want to be with a man that controls me, beats me, and abuses me.

Which number describes the type of relationship that you want? _____

Most women pick number 1 because that's how they want to be treated. When you know your worth you don't settle for number 2, 3, 4 or 5 you settle for number 1. Starting today settle for number 1 only. Don't settle for anything less than what you're looking for. Don't settle for anything less than what your worth. Knowing your worth requires you to REJECT all men who treat you like number 2, 3, 4 and 5. From now on I want you to only accept a man that treats you like the Queen that you are.

Dear me. From now on I will reject all men who don't treat me like number 1. I know my worth, and I know what I'm looking for. If a man isn't treating me how I want to be treated I will move on. If I accept number 2, 3, 4 or 5 I'm settling for less, and I don't know my worth. Starting today I will no longer settle for less.

Would you want your friend, son or daughter to be with a number 2, 3, 4 or 5?

If not, why do you stay with them? Start loving yourself today. Treat yourself right.

STEP 14: KEEP YOUR HEAD UP HIGH

A Queen walks around with her head up high, and her shoulders back because holding her head down will cause her crown to come tumbling down. Some women walk around with their head down looking at the ground. Walking with your head down is a sign of low self-esteem. A confident woman stands tall and walks with her head up high. A confident woman walks like she is the star of her own hit show, and guess what she is the star of her own show. Realize that you're the star of your life. You're playing the leading role, and it's your job to make sure that your life story is as good as it can be. Next time you go out into public, hold your head up high and stop worrying about what others think of you. You have the right to hold your head up high, and you have the right to do whatever you want with your life. Walking with confidence attracts men because men are attracted to women who love themselves. If runway models walked with their head down the show wouldn't be a success, and people would know that they weren't confident. When you walk with your head down it makes you look like a miserable person, and most people don't want to hang around miserable people. If you walk into a room with your head up high, and a smile on your face people will be drawn to you. If you walk into a room moping around, with your head hanging down people will avoid you because you look like a party pooper. Life isn't as bad as you think, and not everyone is hung up on looks. Just be yourself, and people will fall in love with the real you.

From now on will you walk with your head held high, like the Queen that you are? _____

Activity 16

Go to a store and smile, wave or say 'hey' to 5 random people.

Write down what happened?

This activity will show you that most people respond to you based on how you are responding to them. A friendly smile, wave or hey will probably get you the same in return. It will also show you that everyone around you isn't going to be rude to you because of how you look. In fact, most people are quite understanding because they have flaws of their own. Only superficial people will hate you because of your flaws, and you don't need superficial people in your life anyway.

Activity 17

The next time you're at a store look around to see what everyone else is doing.

What you'll notice is that most people are focused on their own life, and they're only focused on what they came to the store for. If they look at you, it will only be for a second, and then they will return back to what they are doing. People with low self-esteem tend to think that everyone is focusing on them, after them or looking at their flaws, but they should realize that everyone isn't. Once you see that other people aren't as focused on your flaws as much as you think they are you'll be more relaxed in public. In reality, you're the one that's focused on your flaws, and you're looking around to see who will make fun of your flaws or who will be mean to you because of your flaws. Stop looking around for negativity, and start creating some positivity. You're looking around for people that are going to be negative towards you instead of just focusing on what you came to do. Start having a positive attitude when you go out. Look for people that are being nice to you, give a smile to those who glance, stare or look at you. Give people who look at you in a rude way a smile. A simple smile will let rude people know that you're okay with yourself and if they have a problem with how you look that's their problem, not yours.

Realize that if someone doesn't like you, the way you look or the way you live your life that it's their problem not yours. Hold your head up high, Queen, because you're the star of your life.

STEP 15: REALIZE THAT IT'S NOT GOING TO KILL YOU

1. People staring at you won't kill you.
2. People making fun of you won't kill you.
3. People hating the way you look won't kill you.
4. People not liking you won't kill you.

So, stop acting like those things are going to kill you. People have made fun of you before, but you're still alive, and what they said or did to you didn't kill you. Sure it can hurt, but it won't kill you. If you go to a store and everyone stares at you it's not going to kill you. If your enemies don't like you or how you look it's not going to kill you.

If something isn't going to kill you it isn't worth stressing over. Realize that what they don't like about you or your life ISN'T your problem; it's their problem so let them find a way to solve their own problems or ignorant issues. From now on don't stress over things that aren't your problem. Whether they like you or not your life will still go on and on and on.

Rachel hates being in public places because people stare at her. She thinks people are staring at her flaws, and judging her because of them. So, she stays home, and hides from everyone. Her fear of being stared at is ruining her life, causing her to be unhappy, and holding her back in life.

Why is Rachel letting something that isn't' going to kill her ruin her whole life? If people stare at her or hate her because of her flaws they're ignorant, and she doesn't need them in her life anyway. Rachel needs to just live her life, and be herself. Once she accepts herself for who she is, and stop hiding from the world her life will change for the better. Rachel needs to realize that people staring at her isn't what's ruining her life. What's ruining her life is her dislike of herself. People staring at her isn't killing her physically, but her stressing over their stares is killing her emotionally. Rachel doesn't like herself, so she hides herself from the world. Rachel hates her flaws so she stays away from people that might judge her because of her flaws. When people stare at Rachel she invents things that they might be thinking, and she imagines them saying hurtful things to her. In reality, the things she thinks others are thinking is what she thinks of herself. Plus, she is assuming that others are thinking the same negative thoughts that she is. Everyone that looks at Rachel is automatically her enemy because she assumes that they will dislike her or judge her because of her flaws. Someone could just glance at her for a few seconds, and she would imagine them saying all kinds of negative things about her; when in reality they might not have thought any of those things at all. If Rachel went out in Public without thinking negatively or assuming the worst about people she would realize that being around others isn't so bad. In fact, she'd realize that everyone has flaws, and most people are worried about their own life not hers. Rachel enters into the room with a negative attitude about people she doesn't even know, she judges the very people that she doesn't want to judge her. She needs to realize that she is creating her own problems, and creating unnecessary stress in her life. She goes out looking for problems instead of just enjoying her day.

If what they say or do isn't going to kill you stop letting it ruin your whole life. Rachel is letting her fear of being stared at RUIN her whole life. She doesn't go to parties or other things because of this fear. Don't be a Rachel. Go out and have fun. Stop letting things that won't kill you CONTROL your life. If you want to win against your enemies just smile. Your enemies hate seeing you smile. Your enemies want you to be miserable. So, if you hide yourself, give up on yourself, or hate yourself you're giving your enemies what they want.

1. Should Rachel let her fear of being stared at RUIN her whole life?

2. Should Rachel stay home and hide from everyone or go out and enjoy her life?

3. Are the people staring at Rachel ruining her life or is Rachel ruining her own life because she's afraid of their stares?

The problem isn't people staring at Rachel, it's Rachel not loving herself. It's Rachel hiding behind her flaws, and not wanting other people to see them. It's Rachel giving up on her life, her social life, her goals and other things in life because of her flaws. Realize that the problem isn't always what others think it's what you think of yourself. Your self-worth is determined by what you think of yourself.

Never let a flaw ruin your life or hold you back. Go out and enjoy life as best you can. You only have one life so make the best of it. Being a Rachel is no fun, and being a Rachel requires you to be miserable for the rest of your life. Do you want to be miserable for the rest of your life? If not, you have to start living your life for you, and stop caring about what others think. After all it's YOUR LIFE, not theirs.

STEP 16: LET GO OF NEGATIVE PEOPLE

1. Let go of anyone that doesn't know your worth
2. Let go of people that are bringing you down
3. Let go of people that act like you're not good enough.
4. Let go of people that have too much negative energy
5. Let go of people that are holding you back and making you miserable.

Realize that people who act like you're not good enough don't belong in your life. Holding onto them will damage your self-esteem and lower your self-worth. Their negative energy will drain you and stress you out. Your instincts and emotions are telling you that you need to get away from them, but you keep holding onto them because you want love from the wrong type of people. Let go of them because they are poisonous to your life, and they are stopping you from meeting someone that will bring joy to your life. Let go so you can be free emotionally, mentally, and physically.

Chapter 3: DATING

Chapter 2 was to help you realize your worth, and let you know that you're a Queen. Chapter 3 will go over things in more detail, and prepare you for the dating world.

STEP ONE

Is to decide if you're ready to date. If you've just gotten out of a relationship give yourself time to heal before you start dating again. If you're in the middle of a divorce or you're separated don't start dating until the divorce is final. Don't start a new relationship if you're still trying to get your ex back. Don't start a new relationship to try and get over your ex. Basically; don't search for a new relationship until you're 100% done with the old one. If you do you're going to start the new relationship off on the wrong foot because of all the baggage you're bringing into it. Also, you won't give the new person a fair chance because you'll be too busy focusing on your ex or past problems instead of them.

STEP TWO

Is to examine your past history of men.

What type of men have you dated before?

Did they all treat you the same way?

Well, if you keep dating the same type of men you're going to have the same type of relationships.

What is your type?

Do you only date one type of men?

Start dating other types of men. Start dating men who you feel are compatible with you. Don't date a man because he's interested in you date him because you're interested in him. Some women find a man that isn't compatible with them and then they try to change him into what they're looking for. Find someone that's already what you you're looking for instead of a man that you think you can change into what you're looking for. Be open to dating people outside of your circle. Give nice guy's a chance. After a woman has dated bad boys, nice guy's will seem boring or desperate to her because she isn't used to dating a man that gives her attention without her having to work for it or chase him. Nice guys are always there for you. They don't make you beg for their attention, affection or a commitment. That's the type of guy that you should want to meet. Stop chasing jerks and bad guy's.

STEP THREE

Is to examine the things you've done in previous relationships.

If you keep having the same type of problem in every relationship the problem might be you. Something you're doing or not doing is telling men that it's okay to treat you like that. Something you're looking for in a man is causing you to pick the wrong men. I'm not saying that their bad behavior is your fault, but I am saying that you're allowing some of these things to happen to you.

Below are a few examples of women who allow or cause things to happen to them.

1. Sally sleeps with men on the first or second date. Then she wonders why she is constantly being put in the 'friends with benefits' zone

2. Jasmine never stands up for herself because she doesn't want anyone to be mad at her, and she's afraid to speak up for herself. Then she wonders why men walk all over her.

3. Christy dates men who never offer to take her on real dates. She allows them to come to her house to hangout and she wonders why she's always the booty call instead of the girlfriend.

4. Tasha ignores all the red flags men give her and she puts up with disrespect because she loves them too much to leave. Then she complains about how men treat her.

5. Mandy has sex with men just to get them to like her and she wonders why men don't respect her or take her seriously.

6. Jill breaks her back for men who aren't interested in her just to get them to like her or be with her and she wonders why she's always getting used.

7. Alexus keeps taking her cheating boyfriend back because he promises that he'll stop cheating on her. Then she complains because he keeps hurting her.

8. Marsha goes to the club every weekend and she leaves the club with men she doesn't know. Then she complains that men hit and run her.

9. Sally throws herself at men just because they're hot, and she has sex with them just because they're hot. Then once she gets to know them she complains about their personality and calls them jerks.

10. Tamara spends all of her money on men who never do anything for her just to get them to like her. Then she complains about how men use her for money.

11. Mallory knows John is playing her, but she puts up with it because she thinks she can change him and make him love her.

- What things have you done in the past to try to get a man to like you?

- What things have you put up with in the past just to keep a man around?

- What things do you allow men to do to you that you know aren't right?

They shouldn't have treated you that way, but you shouldn't have allowed them to treat you that way over and over again.

Before you go to step 4, do the following assignment.

Write down 3 things you won't allow men to do to you anymore. Or read the following 3 things out loud

1. **I won't allow men to use me for sex**

2. **I won't allow men to walk all over me**

3. **I won't allow men to disrespect me**

STEP FOUR

Is to examine why you chose to give the men in your past a chance.

What made you want to give Mr. Wrong a chance? What about him interested you? Knowing why you choose the wrong men will help you to stop choosing them.

Never date a man for the following reasons:

1. Never date someone just because they look good. Physical attraction is important, but it takes more than physical attraction to keep a relationship going. What else do they have to bring to the table?

2. Never date a man just because he's rich. Being financially stable is a good thing, but if you don't love him you'll be miserable and the relationship won't last.

3. Never date a man just because you're lonely and he's the only choice you have at the moment. You'll waste his time and yours and you'll end up breaking his heart. Ask yourself, "Am I giving him a chance because I'm interested in him or because I'm lonely?" If you're not that interested just move on.

4. Never date a man just to get laid. Getting laid isn't worth disrespecting yourself for or risking your health for.

STEP FIVE

Is to determine if your past is influencing your dating decisions.

1. Are you giving the men you meet a fair chance at getting to know you?

2. Are you pushing men away because you think they'll hurt you?

3. Are you constantly looking for something wrong with the men you date just so you can push them away?

4. Do you think that all men are the same?

5. Do you think every man you date is going to hurt you?

6. Do you hate men because of the things that have happened to you in the past?

7. Are you afraid to trust men because of the things that have happened to you in your past?

If you answered 'yes' to one of the above questions your past is influencing your dating decisions. You're letting what your ex did to you ruin your chance at finding Mr. Right. You're letting what a few men did to you make you hate every man on the planet. You're afraid to trust men because you've been hurt by a few men. You put up with abuse or disrespect because every man you've dated has treated you wrong. You stay with the wrong men because you're used to being treated wrong.

Realize that there are good men out there. Every man doesn't mistreat women. The men you met were bad, but that doesn't mean that all men are bad. Would it be fair if someone said that all women were bad? No! It wouldn't be fair because you know you're not a bad woman. There are good men out there you just have to go through a few losers to find one. The men in your past shouldn't have hurt you, but you shouldn't let those men ruin your chance at finding a good man. Never let the person who hurt you make you miss out on someone that wants to love you. Never let the person that left you make you miss out on someone that wants to be with you.

Even though you're hurting inside because of your past, you still have a lot of love inside of you. And someone out there will be happy to be loved by you, and they'll be happy to give you all of their love too. But you won't find them until you stop letting your past control your dating life.

Starting today I want you to start giving people a chance instead of pushing them away. Will you give love another chance? You won't find love unless you give some guy out there a fair chance to win your heart.

In my book '22 Steps to Letting Go of the Past' I show you how to let go of the past.

STEP SIX

Is to determine if you have trust issues. After you've been hurt a lot it's hard to trust people. If you've been hurt too much you might think that everyone is out to get you. So, you constantly have this big wall around you, and you do whatever it takes to keep people from hurting you. Inside of those walls is a heart that's been broken by too many people. A heart that can't take any more pain.

People with trust issues want to be loved, but they can't trust anyone so they give up on love.

1. Realize that there are good men out there who have been hurt just like you have, and they are looking for someone to love.

2. Realize that every man isn't a bad man. Have you noticed that some men are great dads and some men are deadbeats? _____

Have you noticed that some men will fight another man just to protect his woman? _____

Yet other men beat their woman like she means nothing to them? Not every man is the same. You just have to find a man that is willing to protect you instead of hurt you. A man that will be a loving husband and a good father instead of a man that will be a horrible husband and a deadbeat dad.

Don't be afraid to give a guy a chance, just take your time and get to know him. If he loses your trust it makes him look bad, not you. It shows that he's dishonest or disloyal. It also shows that he's not the one for you. If someone loses your trust don't bash yourself for falling for them or for believing in them because it's not your fault that they're untrustworthy, dishonest or disloyal. The only thing you did was give him a chance and there's nothing wrong with giving someone a chance. You might regret giving him a chance, but that part of your life is over and done with. You gave him a chance and he messed up. Now, you're moving on to someone else. Just be glad that you finally saw his true colors.

"If you don't learn how to trust again you'll never find love again."

STEP SEVEN

Is to get to know yourself. How can they get to know you if you don't know yourself?

Before going to step eight do the following assignment.

Assignment 2: Answer the following questions honestly.

1. What's your favorite color?

2. Do you hate yourself? If yes, why?

3. What's your favorite food?

4. What's your favorite song?

5. Is anything from your past bothering you? If so, what is it?

6. What makes you cry?

7. What do you regret?

8. Do you love yourself flaws and all?

9. If you could change something about yourself what would it be?

10. What do you like about yourself?

11. Have you ever had a broken heart?

12. Do you hate the person that broke your heart?

13. Did you give up on love because you were hurt?

14. Are you still hurt?

15. Are you angry and bitter because of your past?

16. Are you a nice person?

17. Are you mean or do you pretend to be mean?

18. Do you act mean to protect yourself from getting hurt?

19. Do you want to fall in love or do you hate love?

20. Do you miss anyone?

21. What really makes you mad?

22. What always makes you smile?

23. What's your worst memory?

24. What's your best memory?

25. If you could do anything with your life what would it be?

26. Are you going after your dreams?

27. Do you believe in yourself?

28. Do you love yourself?

29. Are you disappointed in yourself? If so, why?

30. Can you change some of your bad habits if you really wanted to?

31. If you tried your best could you get things done?

32. What's your favorite holiday?

33. What are you really good at?

34. What do you suck at?

35. Do you want to change?

36. Are you a good person?

37. Do you put with disrespect just to get love?

38. Do you allow men to hurt you just to keep them around?

39. Do you allow men to use you for sex or money because you want them to like you?

40. Do you try to prove yourself to men who act like you're not good enough?

41. Do you chase men who act like you're not good enough?

42. Do you think you can change your life?

43. Why do you put up with the wrong men?

- Is it because you're used to being treated wrong? Every man you've known has done you wrong so you're used to it now. You even expect it.

- Is it to win their love?

- Is it because you think you can change them or make them love you?

- Is it because you don't care about yourself?

- Is it because you love them more than you love yourself?

- Is it because you don't love yourself?

- Is it because you're lonely?

- Is it because you don't think you're good enough to find someone else?

- Is it because of your past?

- Is it because you think they love you?

- Is it because you think they'll like you if you put up with it?

44. Do you want to change your life? _____

Well get up and do it, you can do anything you put your mind to.

STEP EIGHT

Is to set your standards. Some women set their standards too low and some women set their standards too high. If you're looking for a perfect man you'll never find one because perfect men don't exist. If you're not perfect don't expect the one to be perfect. If you set your standards too low, you'll end up dating men who you wouldn't set your enemies up with. When you're looking for a man make sure he's compatible with you. If you just met him and you're already thinking of ways that you can change him he's not the one for you. If he was the one you wouldn't' want to change everything about him.

When you're setting your standards make sure that you meet those standards also. It's not fair for you to expect something that you can't bring to the table yourself.

Before you go to step nine do the following assignment.

Assignment 3: Set your standards

What are 5 things that you're looking for in a man?

What are 5 things you're not looking for in a man?

If you meet a man that doesn't meet your standards don't give him a chance. One of the main problems that women have is that they tend to lower their standards just to get a man.

When some women meet a man who doesn't meet their standards they give him a chance anyway because they think they can change him into the man of their dreams. I call these women Mrs. Fix its because they think they can change Mr. Wrong into Mr. Right. They should realize that no matter how much you try you can never turn Mr. Wrong into Mr. Right. If he doesn't meet your standards when you meet him he's not going to meet them if you get into a relationship with him. What you see is what you get, expecting more leads to disappointment. If you settle for the type of man you're looking for you won't have to change him.

You're a Mrs. Fix it if you do the following

1. When you meet a man your brain automatically thinks of things that you want him to change about himself.

2. The first thing you do when you meet a man is think of things you want to change about him.

3. When you first meet a man you start thinking of ways that you can help him with his problems.

4. You meet a man you're not that interested in but you give him a chance anyway because you think you can fix him up

5. You settle for a sorry man and try to turn him into a real man

6. You just met a guy and you're already trying to change him, make him love you or make him do things he isn't doing on his own.

7. You settle for men with more baggage than an airline because you think you can help them fix all of their problems

8. You let men treat you wrong because you think you can fix their issues and make them treat you right.

9. You think you can stop a man from hurting you, using you or abusing you by showing him more love and fixing his issues.

10. You give men a chance because you think you can work with what they've got even though they don't have much to work with.

Find a man that doesn't need to be fixed up.

If Mrs. Fix It doesn't have to make a man love her or fix him up she loses interest in him. She's not used to having a good man she's used to men that she has to fix. She's used to men that she has to make love her. She's used to men that she has to take care of. She's used to men who don't take care of her needs. If you're a Mrs. Fix it you need to stop settling for men that make you do all of the work, and find a man that is willing to take care of you too.

"Some women settle for less, then they try to change it into more"

"If you have to lower your self-worth just to be with him you shouldn't be with him"

"If you have to lower your standards to barely anything just to be with him you shouldn't be with him"

"If you just met him and you already want to change a million things about him he isn't the one for you"

STEP NINE

is to love yourself flaws and all. We all have stuff we hate or dislike about ourselves, but we should never let those things make us hate everything else about ourselves. I mean there are plenty of good things about you too, and that's what you should be focusing on. Focus on how smart you are, how talented you are at something, how good of a mom or dad you are. How good of a friend you are, how nice you are, how good you are at cooking or learning new things. There are so many good things about you so never forget that. Never let a few flaws make you hate everything else about yourself. The people that love you won't care about your flaws anyway, and if someone doesn't like you because of your flaws they're ignorant and judgmental. And who needs an ignorant person in their life anyway? Always remember that there's more to you than just your looks and the people that love you won't care about your flaws.

From now I want you to give yourself 3 compliments every time you look in the mirror. I want you to stop putting yourself down because it's not fair to you. Never put yourself down or bash yourself. It's not right when other people bash you, and it's not right when you bash yourself. If you're constantly bashing your own looks you are your own bully, and you're being cruel to yourself. Treat yourself the same way that you want others to treat you. Starting today you need to start giving yourself some compliments and stop bullying yourself. Show yourself some freaking love. Stop treating yourself like crap. Before we go to step 6, tell me 3 good things about you. Don't go to step 6 until you do. Also, every time you catch yourself bashing yourself I want you to give yourself a compliment. Replace all of your put downs with compliments.

When someone makes fun of you I want you to realize that what they're saying about you isn't about you. They could care less about your flaws because your flaw doesn't affect them in anyway. When they make fun of you it's for one of the following reasons.

They are jealous of you - *They're jealous of your looks, success, relationship, wealth, popularity or anything else that you have that they don't have.*

Your flaws make them feel better about their own flaws - *They make fun of people who have more flaws than they have so they can feel better about their own flaws.*

They're bitter- *They're hurting inside or they're angry and they want someone to take their anger out on.*

For attention or Popularity -*This person bashes you or makes fun of you for attention or popularity. They usually do this in front of a group of people for laughs or attention.*

All of the above reasons have nothing to do with you; they're just making fun of you for their own selfish reasons. Next time they make fun of you just remember that it's not about you. If they're around a group of people or it's in public just know they're doing it for attention. If you're successful or popular they might make fun of you out of jealousy. If the person acts like they're angry or mad at you they're just taking their anger out on you, and something else is going on in their life. Once you realize that it's not about you it will be easier to deal with people who bash you. Just ignore them because their opinion can't ruin your life or happiness unless you let it. Never let someone else's opinions of you make you hate yourself. Just focus on the people that love you and care about you. Haters and enemies shouldn't control you or your emotions.

"The person in your mirror is counting on you to love them and protect them. Don't let them down!"

"Don't hate yourself because of what your haters say about you"

"Your biggest bully is staring at you every time you look in the mirror."

"Say no to 'put downs' and say yes to 'compliments'"

"The only people that matter is those who love you and support you."

STEP TEN

is to determine your worth. When a woman doesn't know her worth she lets a man tell her how much she is worth.

1. If he treats her like crap she thinks she deserves to be treated like that because of something she did.

2. If he doesn't want to commit to her she thinks that she isn't good enough.

3. If he keeps cheating on her she thinks that the other women must have something that she doesn't have and that she's not good enough for him.

4. If he only wants sex from her she thinks she must not be smart enough, good enough or pretty enough for him to be with.

You should never let a man tell you your worth. You should know that you're good enough without a man having to tell you that you're good enough. If someone doesn't think you're good enough you shouldn't agree with them. Just because they think you're the wrong person for them it doesn't mean that something is wrong with you.

"Next time a man acts like you're not good enough, don't agree with him just move on to someone that thinks you're good enough."

"Once a woman knows her worth she doesn't care if someone doesn't think she's good enough because she already knows she's good enough"

"Once a woman knows her worth she doesn't put up with disrespect because she knows she deserves to be treated better than that"

"A woman that knows her worth doesn't settle for what a man wants unless it's what she wants too."

Some women claim to know their worth, but they're putting up with one of the things below

1. They're letting a man use them for sex.

2. They're letting a man walk all over them.

3. They're letting a man abuse them or beat them

4. They're letting a man cheat on them over and over again.

5. They're letting a man disrespect them.

- If you're letting a man use you for sex you don't know your worth.

- If you're letting a man walk all over you, you don't know your worth.

- If you're letting a man cheat on you over and over again you don't know your worth

- If you're letting a man beat you or abuse you, you don't know your worth.

Actions speak louder than words. So, if you know your worth prove it by not putting up with disrespect.

What are you putting up with just to keep men around?

"What you put up with is what you think your worth"

"If he doesn't think you're good enough to be with, you shouldn't think he's good enough to sleep with"

"Mr. Wrong will keep you around for the wrong reasons"

"You can do everything you can to make the wrong person happy, but they'll only make you miserable"

STEP ELEVEN

is to change the way that you view love. If you've never been loved the right way, it's easy to hate love. If everyone you've ever dated has treated, you wrong your view of love has been tainted and warped into something that it isn't. The real definition of love isn't letting someone use you, walk all over you, abuse you, or disrespect you over and over again. The real definition of love isn't leaving someone you love or cheating on them over and over again. However, when you think of love that's what comes to your mind. Love has become something that hurts you and causes you to feel pain instead of something that cares about you and makes you feel happy. Realize that the love you experienced in the past wasn't real love. If you keep dating you'll find real love one day, but if you give up on love you'll always think that love is something it isn't. What your exes did to you wasn't love so stop calling it that.

Before you go to step twelve do the following assignment

Assignment 6: Answer the following questions as quickly as you can. Don't over think the questions just say the first thing that comes to your mind.

> 1. When someone mentions the word 'love' what's the first thing that comes to your mind?

> 2. When someone mentions the word 'love' what's the second thing that comes to your mind?

If your answers were negative and the word 'love' didn't make you smile your view of love has been tainted. Realize that love isn't a bad thing. You've just been with the wrong people. Once you find the right person your view of love will change into what it should be. What's the real definition of love? Don't accept disrespect and call it love. Don't give love a bad name just because of what your ex or someone else did to you. If you start a relationship with a negative view of love you will set that relationship up to fail.

Also, a lot of people believe that they only get one chance at love, but I believe that you get more than one chance. There are plenty of men in the world that are compatible with you. Some women meet a man and stay with him their whole life. Some women marry three men in their lifetime. Some women have a few long term relationships that made them happy for as long as it lasted. Don't hold onto Mr. Wrong because you think he's the only man you'll ever like. Think about the men you've liked or loved in your past. At the time you thought they were the one or someone really special, but then you moved on and found another guy. There will always be someone else out there for you, you just have to find them.

STEP TWELVE

is to stop thinking that you need a man to be happy. Having a man in your life should be a bonus not a requirement. Some women jump in and out of relationships because they can't stand to be alone. No-one wants to be lonely, but jumping into bed or relationships with men just to get rid of loneliness will lead to you getting hurt a lot. There's a big difference between falling in love and jumping into a relationship because you're lonely. When you're single you should be focusing on yourself and getting your life together. Then when you find a man you'll be ready to share your life with him. Some women think they need a man in order to feel complete. Don't look for someone to complete you, complete yourself or you'll feel empty when they leave. If you think you need a man to complete you, you don't know your worth. Saying that you need a man to complete you is saying that you're worth 100 percent when you're with him and 50 percent without him. A man should complement you not complete you.

STEP THIRTEEN

Is to not put up with disrespect. Just because you love someone it doesn't mean that you should let them walk all over you or disrespect you. People know who they can walk over and who they can't. So, if someone is walking all over you it's because they know you'll put up with it. If you needed to borrow something right now who would you call? If you wanted to go out right now who would you call? When I asked you who you would call someone's name popped into your head because you know that person will say 'yes' to you. Well, when a user or player wants something your name pops up into their head and they call you because they know you'll say 'yes', and they know you'll put up with it.

Do you know someone that you would never yell at? Do you know someone that you yell at sometimes? Everyone knows who they can do certain things with and who they can't. You can yell at a family member, but you know you can't yell at your boss. What's the difference between your boss and your family member? Your boss demands respect and your boss won't put up with your crap. Also, if you yell at your boss you won't get away with it. On the other hand, your family member will put up with it, and you'll get away with it. Players and users walk all over you because you put up with it, and you let them get away with it. They don't respect you. If you accept their disrespect they'll never respect you.

If you want respect, put your foot down, speak up for yourself and tell them what you won't put up with.

Below are a few examples of people getting walked over because they don't demand respect.

1. Tim calls Melissa every night after he leaves the club because he wants to get laid. He knows that she'll let him come over even though it's 2 am. Melissa is just his booty call and he's not interested in being with her.

2. Jim didn't show up for his date with Mandy because he wanted to hang out with his friends. He didn't call her to tell her that he wasn't coming he just stood her up. The next day he called her at 9 Pm because he wanted to get laid and she let him come over.

3. Craig isn't interested in Tasha, but he likes having sex with her. He never calls her to see how's she's doing, and he never helps her with anything. He just uses her for sex. Tasha feels used, but since she likes Craig she lets him use her body. She's hoping that he'll be with her one day.

4. Max has cheated on Constance twice. When he cheats he apologizes to her and she takes him back. Since he knows she will put up with his cheating he is planning on cheating again. He knows that he can cheat as much as he wants too and she still won't leave him. When he gets caught he'll get yelled at, but he won't lose her.

5. John hangs out with Toya at night time only. He comes over, watches a movie, and has sex with her and then he leaves as soon as sex is over. Toya puts up with it because she thinks she can make him fall in love with her.

6. Jack only calls Jill when he wants something, but she gives him what he wants just to make him happy. She thinks he'll fall in love with her if she makes him happy.

7. George goes in and out of Sue's life. Sometimes he acts interested in her and sometimes he acts like she doesn't exist. Sue lets him go in and out of her life because she loves him.

If you have to put up with disrespect just to be with them, you shouldn't be with them. Don't accept disrespect just to keep them in your life.

STEP FOURTEEN

is to get yourself together. Men are looking for women who have their own life. They also want a woman that keeps herself together and acts like a lady. Make sure you take care of your hygiene, and you look feminine at all times.

Before you go on a date:

1. Make sure your breath is fresh

2. Make sure you don't have body odor

3. Make sure your nails are presentable and clean

4. Make sure you're not revealing too much or showing too much skin

5. Make sure your clothes are clean and neat

6. Make sure you smell feminine

STEP FIFTEEN

is to date around. You can't find Mr. Right if you never date. Most women are single because they're wasting all of their time on a guy that doesn't belong to them. They're wasting all of their time on Mr. Wrong when they should be out there trying to find Mr. Right. If Mr. Wrong wanted you he would have claimed you already. He hasn't claimed you because he doesn't think you're Mrs. Right. Go out there and date as many guys as you like just don't sleep with them. The more guys you date the better your chances of finding someone. Keep dating until you find a guy that wants more than just sex from you. Men are competitors if they want you they'll claim you before anyone else can.

.

STEP SIXTEEN

is to take your time and get to know him.

Ask Real Questions.

If you decide that you want to give him a chance start asking real questions. Real questions are things you need to know to find out if he's compatible with you. What's his religion? Does he do drugs? What does he think about cheaters? What are his views on Abortion? Ask questions that will reveal his morals, his beliefs and his true colors. Some people ask basic questions and then they act surprised when they don't know anything about the guy. Basic questions are "What's' your favorite color or favorite food?" It's good to know his favorite color but how's that going to help you find out who he really is and how he thinks or acts? What are some deal breakers for you? Ask questions to see if he violates those deal breakers. Interrogate him like you're a police officer because if this man is going to be around you and you're going to trust him with your body and heart you should know as much as possible. To really get to know him you have to talk to him face to face or over the phone because texts lack emotion. Players love testing because they have plenty of time to think of an answer and you can't tell if they're being sincere or not. Would you rather hear the words "I love you" or see the words "I love you" in a text? Most people would rather hear it because texts lack emotion and sincerity. Players will hate deep questions, and they will hate getting to know too much about you because they prefer action. To avoid getting played, keep your legs closed and ask real questions. If he doesn't like your questions or he avoids you or stops talking to you cut him off. The right guy will love chatting with you and getting to know all about you. Also, make sure you don't ask questions that are too personal too fast. Real questions are about his interest not his personal life and things he has to trust you to tell you. Men don't get too personal until they trust you.

Get to know him

When you first meet a guy he will only show you what he wants you to see, and usually that's his good side. Almost every guy you meet will make a good first impression, but only a few will make a good lasting impression. A player will act like he's a nice guy when you first meet him that's why you have to take your time and get to know men before you sleep with them. A player will say all the right things, and do all the right things just to get you in bed, and to keep getting you into bed. When you first meet someone you like them because you only know good stuff about them, you only know what they tell you and show you. You don't know anything bad about them so of course you like them. If I only knew good stuff about everyone I would like everybody. However, once you spend time with some people and get to know them you start seeing their bad side or true colors, and you decide that you don't like them. Until you've seen the new guy's bad side, until you've seen him have a bad day, until you've seen how he acts when he's mad at you, and until you've been in an argument with him you don't know him. Don't tell me you know him until you've seen all sides of him

Be his friend first

When you meet a guy don't rush into anything physical. Take your time, and get to know him. Getting close to him emotionally and mentally should be your main goal. Let him get to know your personality, and who you really are. See if he is even worth sleeping with. In order to connect with him you have to connect with the head on shoulder not the head in his pants. He has to see you as a person, and as a friend instead of a sex object. Getting to know a guy and being his friend helps you to connect with him on an emotional level. If you leave out this important stage he might neglect your emotional needs, and then you'll be stuck with a man that wants sex from you, but doesn't try to get to know you. If a man isn't trying to get to know who you really are, and he only seems interested in sex or physical things move on.

STEP SEVENTEEN

is to not rush sex. Some women sleep with the new guy before they've seen all sides of him. The first few dates are way too early to be sleeping with someone, if you do you're just sleeping with a stranger. Then these women say that the guy changed right after sex or he wasn't who they thought he was. These women slept with him because of the good side he was showing them, but if they had waited a little while longer, and asked the right questions they might have seen some of the bad stuff he was hiding. So, they sleep with him because of the good stuff he's showing them and because of how he looks. Then once they sleep with him they feel close to him because of the hormone Oxytocin that is released during sex. Oxytocin makes you feel close to someone and it's known as the bonding hormone. When Oxytocin is released she feels connected to a guy she barely knows, and who barely knows her. Since, she feels connected to him physically she sticks around and tries to connect with him on an emotional level. She also tries to get him to act like he did at the beginning. She loves how he acted when she first met him. However, she has to realize that the guy she first met is the same guy she's with now; she just never got to know him. She slept with him when she only knew the good stuff about him. That's how a woman gets stuck with a man who she's connected to physically, but not connected to emotionally. That's how a woman gets stuck with a man she can't figure out but she feels connected to. That's how a woman gets stuck with a man with a good side that she likes and a bad side that she hates. That's how a woman gets stuck with a man that never planned on being with her and only wanted sex from her. To avoid getting played by men that are only looking for sex you have to connect with a man emotionally before you connect with him physically. Keep your legs closed, ask real questions and wait until he connects with you emotionally before you do anything physical.

Some women think that making a man wait for sex will make him fall in love with them or playing hard to get will make him fall in love with them. Now, that works for guys who are already into you, but it doesn't work for a guy who isn't into you or a player. Making a guy that isn't into you wait for sex won't make him love you or into you. Waiting keeps that guy from being able to use you for sex and it keeps him from wasting your time. If a guy isn't into you nothing you do or say will make him into you. If a guy is into you he'll stick around whether you have sex with him the first night or the fiftieth night. But since you don't know who's into you or not you have to make every guy wait. Waiting won't make him love you but it will make him have more respect for you.

If you throw sex at him just to get him to like you. he'll think you're easy. If you have sex with him without knowing anything about him he won't think your wife or girlfriend material.

STEP EIGHTEEN

is to not have dates at your house or his house. A date at your house or his house is a quick way to get put in the 'friend with benefits' zone. You're telling him that he doesn't have to take you out and treat you like a lady. You're telling him that you're okay with just hanging out and hooking up. If a man doesn't feel as if he had to work to get you he won't think you're worth that much.

Dates are important because it gives you a chance to get to know him, and it also gives you a chance to make memories with him. The first date should be a good memory not a memory that you would be ashamed of.

STEP NINETEEN

is to create memories with him. Creating memories is important because good memories are one thing that people always remember. If you never create memories with him, it will be easy for him to forget you. You don't want sex to be the only thing that pops up in his head when he thinks of you. You want him to think of happy times and the fun things he did with you. So, don't hang out at your place or his place. Hang out somewhere fun and exciting. Do things with him that he's never done before, and you'll be on his mind for the rest of his life.

STEP TWENTY

is to not chase men. If you have to chase a man he isn't the one for you. Men go after what they want. If you're sleeping with a man that doesn't want to commit to you he's telling you what he wants from you and it's just sex. If he wanted more he would ask you for more. When a man is in love with a woman he doesn't want to be 'just friends" with her. Men hate the friend zone. If a man loves you, and you put him in the friend zone he'll be sad and it'll break his heart. So, if a man is happy to be 'just friends' with you he isn't in love with you. When a man is in love with you he'll chase you for months or years just for a chance to be with you. Think about the men you rejected before. Do you remember how much attention they gave you and how desperate they seemed to you? When a man is in love with you he doesn't care how desperate he looks he just wants a chance to be with you and make you happy. If a guy isn't doing everything he can for a chance to be with you he isn't in love with you. Next time you catch yourself chasing after a man remind yourself that he isn't the one for you because if he was he would be chasing you instead. When you first meet a guy he chases you because he wants something from you or he wants a chance to be with you. Think about the guys who chased you in the past. When they wanted you they chased you, but when they lost interest in you they stopped chasing you. Men chase after what they want whether it's sex or a relationship. If he's not chasing you you're not what he wants. If he's only chasing you for sex you'll know it because that's the only thing that he'll want from you.

"Some women get played because they chase after men that are pulling away from them. If he stops calling, testing or coming around don't chase him. Just move on."

STEP TWENTY-ONE

is to not throw yourself at him. Men don't like clingy women or women who don't have their own life. Keep your friends and your hobbies. Also, don't call or text him all day long. Let him miss you sometimes. Don't play hard to get, but don't be too available either. Instead of answering his text a minute later make him wait sometimes. Instead of answering all of his calls let it go to voice mail sometimes. If he hasn't claimed you yet you should still be making him chase you. Don't ignore him; just don't answer him right away. Don't cancel girl's night just to hang out with him. If he thinks he has already caught you even though he hasn't committed to you yet he'll stop chasing you and just relax. Keep him on his toes.

Making a guy wait for your call or text will drive him crazy. Make him wait between 5 - 30 minutes for a response from you and you'll notice a big difference in his behavior towards you. Don't make him wait every time though, keep changing it up. Send his call to voice mail sometimes and at other times answer it on the second ring. Never let a guy think that you are just waiting around for him. Let him know that you have a life with or without him. You might be really into him, but don't let him know that until he gets to know you better and you know he's into you. Let him tell you he has feelings for you first. When a man is into you he'll take you off the market. Some women tell a man that they have feelings for him before the man is into them. Don't rush him; give him some time to get to know you.

A man will stay in a woman's friend zone for years trying to get a chance with her. WHY? That's the one woman he can't have, and that's the woman who refuses to have sex with him. Plus, he has gotten to know her personality and other things about her. So, he already feels connected to her mentally and emotionally. She's still a challenge to him. Most men are in some girl's friend zone and they're trying to get out of it. Be a challenge don't be easy.

Men don't like easy girls, they like a bit of a challenge. Just don't play games.

Men like to sleep with easy women, but when it's time for them to choose a mate they would rather choose someone that was more of a challenge.

I HAVE 2 CARS YOU CAN CHOOSE FROM:

You have to work hard to get car #1

You only have to work a little bit to get car #2

Which car do you really want?

Which car would you think was worth more?

Which car would you appreciate more?

Most people would think car #1 was worth more and that car #2 was something cheap that anyone could get. Since, I was willing to let them have car #2 for a little bit of work they wouldn't think that it was worth much. They also wouldn't appreciate car #2 as much as they would car number #1 because they didn't have to work hard to get it. People appreciate things when they have to work hard to get it. Even though I didn't tell you which car was better you still chose car #1 because you had to work harder to get it. Even if you did choose car #2 you'd still be interested in going after car #1 because it's a challenge to you, and you think it's better. Always be car #1!

A spoiled child doesn't appreciate every toy they receive, but a child who has to earn their toys by doing chores appreciates their toys.

Men will tell you that they refuse to chase a woman, but most of the emails I get from men are about a girl that has friend zoned them, and they want to know how to win her over.

Basically, if a man is into you he'll do anything to be in your life and he'll chase you for years just to win your heart. If he isn't into you he won't chase you, and nothing you do or say will make him fall in love with you. If you have to chase a man that's a sign that he's not into you.

STEP TWENTY-TWO

is to never give up on love. Just because it didn't work with your ex it doesn't mean that it won't work with your next. Have you ever left a job you hated only to land a job that you loved? Well, the past doesn't always predict your future. The right guy is out there waiting for you, but you won't find him unless you keep dating. Always remember the good times, and learn from the bad times. You might not have found love in your past, but you have learned from your past. Never let an ex make you give up on love or life. Never become bitter because of your ex. Your ex is moving on with their life and it's time for you to move on too.

"Strong people don't give up on love no matter how many times they've been hurt"

"People are going to hurt you, but don't let it make you bitter, and don't give up on finding someone better."

STEP TWENTY-THREE

is to speak your mind.

1. Don't be afraid to tell a guy what you're looking for.

2. Don't be afraid to tell a guy that you have feelings for him. If he's into you your feelings for him won't scare him away unless you just met him. If he doesn't feel the same way that you do don't think something is wrong with you just realize that he's wrong for you.

3. Don't be afraid to put your foot down and tell him how you feel.

4. Don't be afraid to voice your opinions even if he doesn't agree with you.

5. If he does something wrong call him out on it.

If you don't speak your mind and stand up for yourself, he'll think that he can disrespect you. Then he'll start walking all over you. Don't be his doormat.

"Men respect strong women, and they walk over weak women who don't stand up for themselves"

If you allow him to do it, he'll keep on doing it

STEP TWENTY-FOUR

is not to settle for less.

- Have you ever settled for less than what you're looking for?

- Have you ever settled for less and then try to change it into something more?

- Have you ever settled for what a guy wanted instead of what you wanted?

The biggest problem that some women have is that they don't stick to what they're looking for. They just settle for what the guy wants. If the guy is just looking for sex they stick around and give him what he wants instead of just looking for another guy.

What are you looking for right now?

1. A fling

2. A booty call

3. A friend with benefits

4. A committed relationship

5. Nothing because you gave up on love

6. Nothing because you're focused on your own life

7. Nothing because you're taking a break from dating

8. Nothing because I'm afraid that I'll get hurt

What number did you choose? The number you chose is what you're looking for. Stick to that number until it changes into something else.

1. If you're looking for a committed relationship don't settle for just sex.

2. If you're looking for 'sex' find men who are looking for just sex instead of men that are looking for a relationship. Don't lead men on that are looking for a relationship.

3. If you're not ready for a relationship right now don't feel as if you have to be in one. There's nothing wrong with trying to get your life together before you add someone else into the picture. Just make sure that you tell people that you're not looking for a relationship.

4. If you have trust issues work on it before getting into a relationship.

Always be honest with what you're looking for, and always stick to what you're looking for. If they don't want the same things you want don't stick around. Some women stick around because they think they can change a man into what they're looking for. Don't try to change Mr. Wrong into Mr. Right just move on to someone else.

Also, most of the people who aren't looking for a relationship would change their mind if they met someone they were really interested in. So, the above numbers can change at any time.

Don't be afraid to ask a guy where you stand. It's your life and it's your body. So, you have the right to know where you stand with him. Some women just listen to what the guy wants and they're afraid to speak up about what they want. Realize that you're the boss of your life, and you have the right to know where you stand with him. If you're afraid to talk to him, you shouldn't be sleeping with him. Communication is the most important part of a relationship. If you're afraid to talk to men about things you're going to get walked over a lot. Start standing up for yourself and what you believe in.

"If you have to ask where you stand. Chances are you're not a priority because if you were you'd know it."

"If you take away the sex what else do you have with that person? If it's nothing, then you know where you stand."

STEP TWENTY-FIVE

You only get one body. Even though you might dislike some things about your body you should still take care of it. A woman's body was beautifully created by God. If you can have children you will carry your children in your womb, and you'll be able to provide them nourishment once they're born with the milk your body makes. Realize that your body is special, and that every time you have sex with Mr. Wrong you're giving him a part of you. You're letting him enter inside of a place that should be sacred to you. A place where only someone that truly loves you, and cares about you should enter. Once a woman loves herself she'll only want to share her body with someone that is willing to share their life with her. Realize that you'll never run out of men that want to sleep with you. Finding a man to sleep with is easy. What you want is a man that wants to be with you, and stay faithful to you. Not a man that just wants sex from you. I don't care how good the sex is if you're sleeping with Mr. Wrong you're giving a special part of yourself to a man that doesn't love you or deserve to enjoy your body. From now on if a man wants to enjoy your body or your bed he has to step up to the plate because you will no longer allow just anyone to enter inside of you. If you've allowed men to use your body or mistreat it, it's not too late to change. Just start respecting yourself, and stop having sex with men who refuse to step up to the plate. If you're sleeping with Mr. Wrong and you have feelings for him tell him how you feel. If you don't he'll think it's okay to have sex with you with no strings attached. Since you're giving him apart of you, you have the right to know where you stand. Where you stand shouldn't be a secret that only he knows. Always remember that it's your life, and you have the right to know what his plans are for you. If he's sleeping with you, and wants to continue sleeping with you he should step up to the plate. If he wants you he needs to commit to you, if he doesn't want you he needs to stop wasting your time. Never stay with a man that wants to sleep with you, but not be with you. He's basically saying that you're good enough to sleep with, but not good enough to be with. If you think that's okay you don't know your worth. If he wants a sex toy or a blow up doll tell him to go buy one because you're a woman and you're not to be played with. It's your life, and your body and if he wants to be in either of them he needs to buy the whole package, and stop sampling the goods. Don't be afraid to tell him what you want. Stop settling for the type of relationship that he wants. If you don't want what he's offering you, tell him you want more. Stop letting him cheat you out of what you want. Also, if you can't talk to him about your feelings you shouldn't be sleeping with him in the first place. It doesn't make sense that you can have sex with him, but you can't talk to him about personal things. I know you might be afraid of rejection, but realize that if he rejects you that he's wrong for you. Plus, if he rejects you, you can finally get Mr. Wrong out of your life. The sooner you have this conversation the sooner you can get the type of relationship that you want or the sooner you can kick him to the curb. Chances are if you're that afraid to tell him you already know where you stand. Your instincts and common sense are telling you that he isn't into you. So, you're afraid to tell him how you feel. However, Mr. Wrong isn't afraid to tell you what he wants, and he makes sure he gets what he wants. The wrong person will never give you what you want, but they'll make sure they get what they want from you. Find out what he wants from you, and where you stand because it's your life, and you have the right to know. If you tell him how you feel, and he's not interested in you kick him out of your life. If he gives you an excuse for not giving you what you want kick him out of your life. From now on when a man isn't willing to give you the type of relationship that you're looking for kick him out of your life because he is wasting your time. If you hold onto him he'll never give you what you want anyway, and you'll regret wasting so much time on him.

SET YOUR RULES

A woman should have a list of things she won't do on dates ingrained in her head. Rules that she won't break no matter what. If you don't have rules you'll just go with the flow and you'll end up doing something you regret.

1. No sex on the first date should be a rule

2. Using a condom no matter what should be a rule

3. Not having the first date at your house or his house should be a rule

Write down a list of rules that you don't want to break. Next to each rule write down why you don't want to break that rule. Then follow those rules no matter what.

Example; I will not have sex without a condom because it's dangerous, I don't want to get pregnant, and I'm not married to him. I refuse to put my health at risk for a few moments of pleasure.

Don't break your rules just to get a guy to like you. Once your brain is programmed to follow these rules you won't break them no matter what the guy says or does to you to try to get you to break them.

My List of Rules

1. ._____
2. ._____
3. ._____
4. ._____
5. ._____
6. ._____
7. ._____
8. ._____
9. ._____
10. ._____
11. ._____
12. ._____
13. ._____
14. ._____

SEX AND RESPECT

Answer the following questions truthfully.

1. How fast do you have sex with the men that you meet?

2. Do you have sex with them before you get to know them?

3. Do you have sex with men to try to get them to like you?

4. Do you use sex to try to keep a man?

5. Do you let men use you for sex just to get them to like you?

6. Do you have sex with men just to feel closer to them?

7. Do you have sex with men because you just like to have sex?

8. Do you let men pressure you into having sex?

9. Do you let the men you date do whatever they want to do to you just to please them?

10. Do you have sex with men just to please them?

11. Do you have sex with men because you think that's all they want from you?

12. Do you have sex with men just to get love or to feel loved?

13. Were you raped or molested in your past and now you're letting the men you date use you for sex?

15. Do you like sex or do you just have sex to please men?

16. Do you have sex with men who act like you're not good enough to be with just to get them to like you?

16. Do you feel used after you have sex with the men you date?

17. Do you have sex with men just to keep them around?

18. Do you have sex with your ex because you're trying to win him back?

19. Do you think that good sex will make a man love you?

20. Do you perform oral sex on men you've just met or men who have no interest in you or respect for you?

21. Do you allow the men you date to have sex with you without a condom just to please them?

22. Do you have sex with men for money or gifts?

If you answered 'yes' to any of the questions above, you're not respecting your body. You're letting men use you for sex just to get a little bit of attention or affection from them. You're giving men sex just to feel loved or wanted. You're having sex with men too fast just to win them over or to feel close to them. Never use sex to get closer to a guy or to make him like you. A guy can love your good sex and still not love you. Never put your health at risk just to please a man. Your body isn't a toy or a play thing for men. It's your body and you only get one. So, respect it and take care of it.

Will you stop letting men use you and disrespect you?

Do you love yourself enough to respect yourself?

HOW TO AVOID GETTING PLAYED

Have you ever met a guy who you thought was sweet until you got to know him, and by then you were already in too deep? He made you smile for no reason, you stayed up all night talking to him on the phone and you loved hanging out with him? Then after you spent a lot of time with him he changed and you realized that he was a jerk or you realized that he wasn't that into you? Wouldn't it be great if you knew he was a jerk the first week instead of months or years later? I mean who wants to waste months or years on a guy who doesn't plan on committing to them or taking things to the next level? Wouldn't it be great if you knew he was Mr. Wrong on the first date instead of finding out AFTER he breaks your heart? I mean it's easy to cut off a jerk on the first date, but once you're in love with one it can be hard to cut him off. I would rather know he was a player before I gave him my all, and before he ripped my heart out because heart break sucks. Well, here's the good news there are over 100 signs that will tell you if he's a jerk before he breaks your heart, and if you know these signs and spot them you won't get played. The easiest way to avoid getting played is simply not to date, but who wants to be alone forever? If you keep getting played you're ignoring these signs over and over again. Chapter 4 will give you a list of signs that he's Mr. Wrong before he can get a chance to break your heart. You'll find out if he's a player before he gets a chance to play you. A lot of these signs will be noticeable before or right after your first date with him. I will also tell you a few things you need to know about players because you have to know these things to avoid them. If you follow these tips you won't get played, and you'll stop wasting time on Mr. Wrongs. Instead of wasting Months or years to find out that he's not into you; I'll tell how you can find out after a few dates or before the first date in Chapter 4.

CHAPTER 4: HOW TO AVOID GETTING PLAYED

REALITY VS. FAIRY TALES

Most girls want to find the right guy, get married, and have a family. Ever since they were a little girl playing with Barbie's they dreamt of the day that prince charming would come into their life, sweep them off their feet, fall in love with them and marry them. They dreamed of their wedding day, and the nice dress they would wear, with the lace veil and the flowing white train. However, as time went on most of those little girls realized that reality was way different from all of those fairy tales they were told. They realized that some men were pretending to be prince charming, but they were really just a frog. A frog that never turned into a prince no matter how much she loved him or kissed him. They also realized that every love story doesn't have a happy ending. Some women waste too much time on Mr. Wrong, because they think they can change him into Mr. Right. If they just love him a little bit more, if they just do all the right things, if they're always there for him then maybe he'll realize that they're the one for him. Are you holding onto reality or a fairy tale? Reality is what's really happening to you, it's how they're really treating you, and it's the cold harsh truth. The fairy tale is that your love can change a frog into a prince, that you can make him love you, that you can make him be with you, that you can make him treat you right, and that you can prove that you're good enough for him. Are you holding onto what's really happening (reality) or what you want to happen (the fairy tale)? The first step to avoid getting played is to face reality no matter how much it hurts. Always deal with what's really happening and how they're really treating you. Don't ignore the truth or try to change it into something that you can handle just accept it. When people can't handle the truth they try to change it or they make up excuses for what's happening to them. To avoid getting played you have to move on when you spot the signs that he's wrong for you. If you don't move on when you spot these signs you'll get played and waste your time on Mr. Wrong. They say "love is blind" and I say love sees everything, but it ignores what it sees. When you see these signs will you ignore the truth or will you accept that he's not into you? They can't play you unless you ignore these signs. In fairy tales you follow your heart, but in reality you have to use common sense and logic to make decisions. Your heart will always try to change your mind, but your mind knows what's best for you.

IMPORTANT STEP

To avoid getting played you have to learn how to handle the truth, how to handle rejection and how to love yourself. Accept the truth no matter how much it hurts. The truth hurts, but believing the lie makes you look foolish, and you'll still end up getting hurt. When someone rejects you or acts like you're not good enough for them, move on. Once you learn how to handle rejection you'll move on as soon as you realize that someone isn't into you. If you don't learn how to handle rejection, you'll chase people that aren't into you and you'll try to make them love you. Chasing someone that isn't into you is a waste of time and it leads to heart break. Also, you have to love yourself enough to know that you deserve a good man. If you're a nice girl you should be someone's girlfriend not someone's, booty call, side chick or friend with benefits. To avoid getting played you have to stick to what you're looking for and never settle for anything less than a real relationship. If someone isn't looking for what you're looking for cut them off because they're wasting your time. Remember who you are and know your own worth. Never let a man walk all over you and never let a man use you or your body. If a man doesn't think you're good enough to be with he isn't good enough to sleep with, and he's wasting your time. Most women are single because they're chasing after Mr. Wrong. They're wasting all of their time and loyalty on a guy that doesn't belong to them, and doesn't want to commit to them. If you want to find Mr. Right you need to stop chasing after Mr. Wrong.

THE NEW GUY

When you meet a guy ask yourself "Am I giving him a chance because I'm lonely or do I really want to get to know him?" Sometimes you don't even like Mr. Wrong when you first meet him; something about him tells you that it just won't work. You don't seem compatible, he acts sketchy, he doesn't seem genuine, or his lifestyle or something else doesn't sit well with you. Basically, your instincts are trying to tell you that something is up, and you should listen. However, there's a big difference between instincts or logic telling you that he isn't compatible and you just being afraid of love or getting hurt. Before you proceed you need to make sure that you're really interested in getting to know him.

NEW GUY CHECK LIST

Make sure he passes all of the things below. If he doesn't move on.

1. His dating profile says that he's looking for a relationship

2. His first message to you was nice and not sexual

3. He keeps the conversations going

4. He talks to you every day or at least every other day

5. He texts you first

6. His first date suggestion is out somewhere not at your house or his

8. He's 100% single

9. You've seen more than 1 picture of him and you know it isn't a fake profile. My advice is to use a free video chat app to meet him, for the first time. Skype is free. Video chatting will allow you to meet him without leaving your home, it will allow you to chat with him to see how the conversation would go in person, to see if there's chemistry and of course to get to know him.

10. He doesn't stand you up for dates

11. When he's out with you he walks besides you and acts like you're his date.

12. He doesn't talk about sex or try to feel on you.

13. He's not putting pressure on you and he's not trying to rush you to have sex.

14. He doesn't keep asking you to come to his house or if can he come to your house.

15. He doesn't call you boo, bae or honey

16. He added you to his Facebook or other social networks

17. He acts the same everywhere you go and around his friends.

18. He's nice to the waitress or waiters

19. At the end of the date he doesn't ask to come over to your place.

20. He doesn't talk about his ex non-stop or compare you to her.

21. He keeps asking you questions to find out more about you.

22. He's not sending you nude pictures or pictures of himself in his boxers.

23. He's local and he's not on vacation, traveling for business or visiting.

24. You've gotten his full name and checked out his Social Media accounts. You can search for his Facebook by using his email, number or full name and city.

25. You've looked him up online, county searches, jail inquiry, google etc. Also, you've right clicked his pictures and performed a google search of his picture

The above sounds crazy but women have found all sorts of information about their potential partners by doing the above searches. Some men were married and others lied about not having children etc. Others had a history of domestic violence or other violent crimes. Some even had scary social media posts and other things that made them a definite Mr. Wrong. Find out about him now, not months later.

YOUR CHECKLIST

Don't do any of the following.

1. Calls and Video chat only, for long conversations. Texting isn't a great way to get to know anyone. Don't text him first. Wait for him to text you first no matter what. After a few weeks you can text him first sometimes. Like a Good Morning handsome text.

2. Don't chase him. If he's into you he'll chase you.

3. Don't have sex with him until he is giving you what you need and taking care of your emotional needs.

4. Don't invite him to your house or go to his house until you've went on at least 5 real dates.

5. Don't be clingy.

6. Don't give him money or pay his bills.

7. Don't drive to see a guy that lives far away. He should be driving to see you or meeting you half way.

8. Don't throw yourself at a guy just because he's hot

9. Don't leave the club with a guy; it makes you look easy and it's dangerous

10. Don't get drunk or have too many drinks with a guy you don't know.

11. Don't agree to have the date at his place, your place, a club or a bar. Real dates only.

12. Don't send him pictures that show too much of your body, especially not nudes.

13. Don't talk about sex.

14. Don't lie just to get him to like you.

15. Don't have sex with him the first night, he's a stranger and he'll label you as easy not wifey.

16. Don't have naked or half naked pictures of yourself on your dating profile

17. Don't write anything in your profile that makes you look like a slut, don't talk about sex either.

18. Don't dress up like a slut for the first date. If a man assumes you're a slut he'll treat you like one.

19. Don't keep looking for the same type of guys OR you'll keep having the same type of relationships.

20. Don't assume that a guy likes you because he wants your number or he likes your body. He might just want sex and that's why you shouldn't rush things until you find out what he wants.

How you act and how you present yourself determines how men will approach you. If you talk about sex too fast he will stop trying to get to know you and focus on having sex with you. If you send him nude and sexy pictures he's going to think you're easy and put you in the sex only zone. If you want him to get to know your personality use your personality to attract him instead of your body.

7 TYPES OF MR. WRONGS

Did he play you or did he just lose interest in you?

Some women confuse Players with men who simply lose interest in them. Some guys are interested in you at first, but once they realize that they aren't compatible with you they leave or they keep you around for sex. If you have sex with him before he figures out what he wants from you, you might get played or left. That's why you should find out what a man wants from you before you sleep with him. Below are 7 types of Mr. Wrongs.

- **Mr. Player** - He is looking for women to play. When he met you he already planned on using you. He isn't looking for anything serious
- **Mr. lost interest** - He was interested in getting to know you, but after he got to know you he left because he didn't think you were the one.
- **Mr. Lead you on** - He lost interest in you, but he still likes something that you're giving him so he's keeping you around for that. He confuses you and makes empty promises.
- **Mr. Jerk** - He acts like he's into you sometimes, but you can tell that he's not that into you because he treats you like shit or acts like you're not good enough for him. He confuses you.
- **Mr. hit and run** - He only wants sex and after he gets it he leaves
- **Mr. Friend with Benefits** - He likes the benefits, he likes hanging out with you, and he thinks you're attractive; but he doesn't think you're the one. He will keep you around until he finds someone that he wants to settle down with.
- **Mr. Booty call** - He only wants sex and he doesn't respect you or care about you.

All of the above Mr. Wrongs will waste your time and they all want sex from you. If you don't want them to play you don't give them what they WANT until you get what you NEED from them.

CATEGORIES

When a guy meets you he's going to observe you and based on his observations he's going to put you into one of the following categories.

- **Friend only, no sex** - He's not attracted to you or he has no choice because you 'friend zoned' him. Or he's attracted to you but he's afraid to tell you how he feels or because you're taken and he knows you're off limits
- **Booty call-** He only wants to have sex with you, he's not that attracted to you, but he likes the sex.
- **Friend with benefits** - He wants to hang out with you and have sex with you. He thinks you're attractive, but he doesn't think you're the one
- **Girlfriend Material-** He thinks you could be the one, but he's not sure yet. He likes a lot of things about you. You're not just sex to him
- **Wife Material-** He thinks you're the one OR could be the one, he thinks you're different from all the other girls.

Guys have a certain image in their head of what the one looks like, how she will act and a list of other qualities. If you don't meet their standards or you don't fit the image that they have ingrained in their head they won't commit to you. However, if they think you're attractive or slightly attractive they will sleep with you because their sex partner standards aren't as high as the wife material standards. If a guy doesn't commit to you it doesn't mean that you're not good enough or that something is wrong with you, it means that he's wrong for you. When you meet the right guy you will fit the image and characteristics that he's looking for. In the mean time you need to cut off these Mr. Wrongs so you can find Mr. Right. Mr. Wrong will only keep you around for the sex, but Mr. Right will keep you around because he wants all of you. Mr. Wrong will give off signs that he is putting you in the 'sex only' categories, and I will give you those signs at the end of this guide. If you spot the signs move on before he uses you for sex, wastes your time and plays you.

FIRST IMPRESSIONS

Girl #1 is wearing a thong and a bra in her profile picture.

Girl #2 is wearing a business suit in her profile picture.

1. If you were a guy which girl would you think was easier?

2. Which girl would you respect more?

3. Which girl would you think would sleep with you on the first night?

4. Which girl would you think your mom would approve of?

First impressions are important. Men will approach you based on how you present yourself. His assumptions might be wrong, but he will go by them until he gets to know you better.

THE CHASE

I went over chasing before, but I'm reviewing it in more detail because I'm noticing that more and more women are doing what a man is supposed to these days.

Some men say they love when women chase them. Don't listen to them! Men were born to hunt; it's in their genetic makeup. Okay, not really, but you get the point. Men tell you that because it makes their job easier, and they like when women throw themselves at them. However, if you chase a man he'll think you're easy and desperate, and not that much of a challenge. He'll love that you made it easy for him to get you, but he'll also think you're easy, and he'll lose interest in you before you can blink your eyes. Don't be surprised when the man you're chasing is still hunting for other women because he's already caught you. Some men say they refuse to chase a woman, but the truth is that most of those man are secretly chasing a girl that has friend zoned them. They have been waiting for months or years for a chance to be with her, and that's exactly what men in love do. They chase and wait for you if they have too. When you meet a player you're a challenge to him until he sleeps with you. When you meet a decent guy you're a challenge to him until he wins your heart. Now, how do you tell who's the player and who's the decent guy? I'll give you some signs later, but for now let's discuss the player. If you have sex with the player he's going to hit and run you or keep you around to use you for sex. If you don't want the player to use you for sex don't give him sex, it's just that simple. You hold the power until you have sex with him. He can't use you unless you're giving him something to use. Don't have sex with him until he connects with you emotionally and wants to take things to the next level. If you have sex with him before you know where you stand you risk getting played. Some guys change right after you have sex with them because sex is all they came for in the first place. They already had you so they don't have to play Mr. Nice Guy anymore. They can just move on to another girl, and call you when they need someone to fall back on or get them off. Never be a guy's booty call or side chick. If you're a nice girl, and you know your girlfriend material you should be someone's girlfriend not someone's booty call, side chick or friend with benefits. Always remember your worth.

SEPARATE SEX FROM EMOTIONS

Just because a guy is attracted to you physically and enjoys having sex with you it doesn't mean that he wants to commit to you emotionally or mentally. A guy can love your sex, but still not love you. To understand a player's point of view you have to realize that they only care about their needs, and they don't care who they have to hurt to get their needs met. If they have to use you just to get off and feel good they'll do it. If you're giving them no strings, no questions asked sex they're going to take it. If you're giving them free money they're going to take it. They know you like them and that you'll do anything for them but that's your problem not theirs because they only care about themselves. If you don't like how they're treating you, leave, but they're going to keep treating you that way, and using you until they're done with you. When someone doesn't love you it's easy for them to hurt you because they don't care about you.

A guy can love your sex and still not love you.

If he's into you, he'll commit to you. If he's keeping you around for sex he won't commit to you.

Some men don't have to like you or even be attracted to you to have sex with you. If you were a player would you rather have sex with a woman you didn't like or use your hands to get off? You would have sex with the woman because it feels better, she might give you head and you don't have to commit to her. If you were a player and women were throwing themselves at you would you turn them down or would you sleep with all of them? You would sleep with all of them, and you'd brag to all of your friends about it later. If you were a player and you didn't like a girl, but she kept giving you sex whenever and wherever you wanted it, no strings attached would you turn her down? Nope, you wouldn't because it feels good to you and you like sex. You might not like her, but you like what she's giving you.

If you're giving a guy benefits with no strings attached he's going to take it, and he's going to keep taking it until you stop giving it to him. If you think a single man is going to turn down sex with a woman think again. He might keep some of the women he has sex with a secret, but he'll still have sex with them. Some men do have standards, but most men have slept with a woman they were not into or attracted to at all just to get off. Most women can't sleep with just any guy. They have to be attracted to him, have chemistry with him or feel a connection to him. Most men don't have to have any of the above to sleep with a woman. All they need is room or place to do it in and they're in. If he refuses to commit to you, but he keeps hanging around you it's because you're giving him benefits, and he isn't going to turn them down. If you think he's going to say no to no strings attached sex think again.

To some men, sex is just sex, nothing more, nothing less. It's just something to do for fun, something that feels good and something to relieve stress. If they're not into you sex with you doesn't mean anything to them, they just want to get off and have fun.

If sex means more to you than that, friends with benefits, and no strings attached sex isn't for you. So, don't settle for those kinds of relationships.

THE JEALOUS PLAYER

Just because he acts jealous it doesn't mean that he loves you. Some men act jealous because they don't want anyone else to sleep with you. They'll try to stop you from dating other people, but they won't commit to you or be with you because their jealousy is just from a bruised ego. They're not jealous because they love you they're jealous because another man is trying to take away their sex, and they feel like they're not taking care of your sexual needs. They think they're not doing a good job if you're out looking for another man. A guy could have 4 women and he'd still want all of them to be with him only. That's just an ego thing not a love thing.

QUICK SUMMARY

To sum things up: To avoid getting played, you have to take things slow, ask real questions, follow your instincts, face reality, keep your legs closed, connect emotionally before physically and cut him off if you spot the signs below. You also have to love yourself, know your worth, learn how to handle rejection and accept the truth even it hurts.

DON'T THINK YOU CAN CHANGE A MAN. IF HE ISN'T WHAT YOU'RE LOOKING FOR OR HE'S NOT OFFERING YOU WHAT YOU'RE LOOKING FOR MOVE ON.

SIGNS THAT HE'S MR. WRONG BEFORE HE BREAKS YOUR HEART

If he does 3 or more of the things below move on because he is Mr. Wrong. He has to do these things BEFORE you have sex with him. If you've already had sex with him, you need to read my book 'Dating Guide for Single Women'. This book is for men you're trying to get to know.

1. **He replies to your questions, but he doesn't ask you questions back.** If he does this to you, don't ask him another question until he asks you something back. If he's into you he'll wonder why he hasn't heard from you, review the conversation, realize what he did wrong and write to you again. If he's not interested in getting to know you he'll let the conversation die out. Some women keep asking questions because they want to talk to the guy, but they should realize that conversations are supposed to be about 2 people getting to know each other not 1 person interviewing another person. If he doesn't text you for days, don't text him. If you miss him don't text him. Let the guy chase you and don't text him first until you're in a relationship with him. Some men are used to women doing all of the work while they just sit back and relax. Make him do the work and he'll see that you're different, and if he wants you he has to come to you because you refuse to chase after a man.

Example; Him: How was your day?

You: Fine and yours?

Him: Good

You: What did you eat for dinner?

Him: Pizza

If he doesn't ask you anything back let the conversation die because he's not interested in keeping it going.

If he's interested in getting to know you he'll realize that it's his turn and he'll ask you something back.

If you keep it going yourself he will get used to you taking the lead and doing all of the work, and soon he won't even text you first anymore.

2. **He acts interested in you but he keeps vanishing** for days at a time then coming back. This guy sees you as an option and he isn't the type that you should take seriously.

3. **You just met him and he's already calling you boo, bae or honey.** Players call you pet names in private to make you feel special, but when you're in public they'll introduce you as a friend or treat you like a friend. They also call you this because they don't know your name or they don't want to call you the wrong name.

4. **He rushes sex.** You just met this guys and he's already trying to feel on you, kiss you and get you to sleep with him.

5. **He's overly sexual.** He flirts with you sexually; he makes sexual comments, sexual jokes and asks sexual questions.

6. **He asks for pictures more than he asks you questions.** He asks you to send him a lot of pictures, but he barely tries to get to know you or ask you questions.

7. **He sends you inappropriate pictures of himself** or pictures of his private parts.

8. **When he asks for a hug he tries to grope you** or push his private parts against you.

9. **He doesn't want to take you on a real first date**. He wants to hang out, chill, come to your place or he wants you to come to his place. Players like to skip the dating stage and go straight to having sex. They're

used to girls that let them have sex on the first date so they think you will do the same if they can just get you alone. Tell the guy that you would rather do something else; if he's interested in getting to know you he'll agree to a real date, if he's not interested in getting to know you he'll try to change your mind or he'll vanish. Some men will tell you to come to their place for a cup of tea or coffee. You don't have to go to a guy's house to get a cup of coffee or tea, you can meet at Starbucks. Always remember that a player wants to get you in bed fast, and he'll always try to find a way to get you to come to his house or to come over to your house. If you don't want to get played, meet him at the dating location instead of having him pick you up. Players like to pick you up, so they'll be at your house at the end of the date. Then they'll ask to use the rest room, they'll say they just want to cuddle or anything else they can think of so you'll invite them in. If you meet him at Starbucks, you can drive yourself home and avoid his sneaky tactics. When the date is over, and you're fixing to leave the dating location the player will ask you what you're fixing to do later because he's still trying to get you in bed. Tell him that you're calling it a night, but you had fun. Always remember that until you connect with a guy emotionally it will be easy for him to let you go and lose interest in you because he doesn't know anything about you and there's nothing connecting him to you. If you haven't connected with him emotionally don't have sex with him. After you've rejected his sexual advances, the player will keep trying to get you in bed or he'll lose interest in you and vanish for a while. A decent guy will realize that you're not that type of girl and he'll respect your boundaries. Once a guy realizes that you're not easy and you're different from other girls he has a little more respect for you. When a guy realizes that you're different that's a good thing.

10. **He takes you on a nice first date, but after the first date he tries to get you to come over to his house** or he wants to come over to your house. After the first date he doesn't want to go on another real date with you. Basically he wants a friend with benefits.

11. **He keeps talking about his ex,** he constantly bashes his ex and he compares you to his ex. Most people talk about their exes just to tell a little about themselves and why they're single, but this guy goes too far. He talks about his exes constantly, compares you to them and bashes them.

12. **He says his exes are crazy and they won't leave him alone.**

13. **He says he isn't talking to any other women, but his phone rings non-stop at all hours,** and you have a feeling that he's lying. Or you've seen girls all over his social profiles.

14. **He asks you if you want a massage or something else that involves him touching you.** Like coming over to cuddle. He wants to do something that could lead to sex.

15. **He tries to get you drunk.** He asks you to meet him for drinks. You should never get drunk on a date with a guy you don't know, it's dangerous and chances are he just wants to get laid. Don't go to bars or clubs with him until you've been on at least 5 dates. Players always try to get you drunk so they can get laid. Just say no to drinks. Don't even have one drink. If he keeps trying to give you drinks or get you drunk end the date because you know what he's up too.

16. **He ignores you in public,** but speaks to you in private.

17. **In private he acts like he's really into you, but in public he acts like you're nobody special.**

18. **In public he keeps a distance between you and him.** When a guy isn't into you he keeps his options open at all times. He will wander around the room; he'll barely get close to you or show you love in public. When you walk with him he'll leave you behind, or drag behind you instead of walking right beside you. Or he'll never leave with you. Basically, he wants other women to know that he's single and

available. When a guy is into you, he stays close to you, he might leave your side sometimes, but most of the time he'll be by you. Also, he'll hold your hand or wrap his arm around you, and walk beside you.

19. **He flirts with other women in front of you.** Most men do look at other women, but they try to sneak and do it. The player doesn't respect you so he will stare at women obsessively and obviously to the point that it embarrasses you. He will turn his whole body around, make comments about her and anything else he pleases.

20. **He doesn't talk about himself or his personal life.** He talks about basic things, but he doesn't try to connect with you. His conversation is basic and you feel like he doesn't want to get to know the real you.

22. **He says that he's getting divorced soon,** he's separated from his wife, he's living with his kid's mom or that he's leaving his girlfriend soon because she doesn't treat him right. Never date a man until he is 100% single. Most of these men are just cheaters and don't plan on leaving their girlfriend or wife anytime soon.

23. **He complains about his financial problems** and he constantly ask you about your job or salary. He jokes about you buying him things to see what you'll say. Believe it or not men can be gold diggers too. If you just met him and he's already complaining about his financial problems, chances are he's looking for a sugar mama. Don't give men money unless you live together or you're in a long term relationship. Don't buy gifts unless it's a special occasion. Most real men don't ask women for money.

24. **When you're talking on the phone with him he keeps rushing off the phone mid conversation.** He hangs up before you get a chance to say goodbye. Chances are his wife or girlfriend is coming home or near him and he has to hang up the phone really fast to avoid getting caught. Some men do this when they're chatting on instant messengers too. This has to happen a lot though.

25. **He only calls you when he's in his car or running errands** because he can't call you when he's at home with his live in girl friend or wife.

26. **He refuses to add you to his Facebook or other social websites.** Or he says he has one but he barely uses it. The latter might be true, but tell him you want it anyway.

27. **He doesn't tell you where he lives.**

28. **He doesn't ask questions to try to get to know you.** He might speak and say hello, but he never asks you real questions about yourself. When you have conversations with him, the conversation is basic and he doesn't talk to you for longer than 5 minutes. When you start to have a real conversation he says he'll call you back later.

29. **He's rushing to meet you but he isn't trying to get to know you.** You're supposed to meet on Saturday, but he barely called you or texted you M-F. This guy doesn't care about connecting with you emotionally just physically.

30. **You haven't heard from him in days, but you keep seeing him online** and then he contacts you again. He's keeping you around as an option.

31. **He keeps standing you up and canceling dates at the last minute.** You're just an option to him.

32. **He cancels nice plans at the last minute and tries to get you to do something not so nice.** For example, you were supposed to have dinner with him. But now he wants you to come to his house and have drinks. If he cancels dinner for going to get a cup of coffee, he might just be low on cash.

33. **You just met him and he's accusing you of lying about things** or lying about being single. Guys do this when they're hiding something; they're just transferring their guilt onto you.

34. **You just met him and you've already caught him in a bunch of lies.** His lying will get worse.

35. **You just met him and he's already trying to boss you around.** Tell you what to wear, how to act, how to do your hair, and how to wear your makeup. He's the controlling type.

36. **He says or does mean or hurtful things then says he's joking.**

37. **He calls you out your name;** bitch, whore or other names then laughs it off.

38. **All of his friends are players** and he hangs around them a lot.

39. **He goes out every night of the week.**

40. **He drowns himself in booze.** He's constantly drunk and you barely see him sober. Sometimes he drives drunk.

41. **He's rough with you.** He acts too aggressive, constantly raises his voice at you or even hits you. He's the controlling, abusive type. He might apologize for his behavior, but he will do it again and again.

42. **Your friends and family warn you about him.**

43. **He loses his temper over small things.** The waiter is taking too long to bring the food so he lashes out at her. You disagree with him and he snaps at you.

44. **He only calls you during the daytime,** at night time you don't hear from him.

45. **He only calls you late at night.** Only after 10.

46. **He never mentions you or says your name online** when he talks about you he doesn't use your user name or real name so no-one will know who he's talking about.

47. **He says he was arrested for domestic violence before but it was his exes fault**

48. **You're on his schedule.** He's too busy for the things you want to do, but he makes times for the things he wants to do. Or he ignores your calls, but he calls you when he feels like it.

49. **He makes up excuses for not calling you back or replying to your text.** Or he says he called or texted you, but he couldn't reach you.

50. **You barely hear from him during the week,** but he blows your phone up to make plans when it's close the weekend.

51. **He shows up HOURS late** when you're supposed to meet him.

52. **He sends you 10 text back to back or calls you 10 times back to back.** This is controlling, obsessive behavior, it will get worse and he will start to get angry when you don't respond fast enough or answer his calls.

53. **He rushes the physical connection but avoids opening up to you emotionally.** This guy is open to sex, but he isn't open to connecting with you on any other level. You'll feel like he isn't opening up to you or trying to get to know the real you. He doesn't seem genuine.

54. **He showers you with compliments.** Compliments are a good thing, but the player will give you a million compliments a day to make you feel special so he can get in your pants. Every other text will have a compliment in it or a pet name.

55. **You just met this guy and he says he loves you or he wants to move in with you.**

56. **You received an email from a guy who says he's really interested in getting to know you, but his profile says that he isn't looking for a relationship.** Don't think you can change his mind just move on.

57. **He asks personal questions, but doesn't want to answer your personal questions about him.**

58. **You meet him when you're out with friends, he asks you what you're doing after, and then he offers to take you home.** He's trying to get laid, and you should never leave with a guy you just met.

59. **He never contacts you first unless he wants to meet up.** This guy put you in the sex zone.

60. **He never text you first**, if you don't text him you won't hear from him.

61. **His Facebook wall is full of girls calling him pet names** or talking to him like he's dating them.

62. **He tries to get you to stop dating even though he though he hasn't claimed you.**

63. **He calls women hoes and bitches.**

64. **He says all women are whores**, or they're all the same but you're different.

65. **He tells you not to fall in love with him.** Or that he's afraid that he'll hurt you.

66. **He says he hasn't had sex in a long time because he's saving his self for the right one and he keeps talking about sex.** You can tell that this guy is lying because he's being too sexual.

67. **He makes empty promises.** He keeps saying that he's going to do this and that for you or with you, but he hasn't done it yet. It might sound sweet when he promises you things, but words don't mean nothing if he isn't backing it up with actions.

68. **He flirts with your friends.**

69. **When you talk about yourself he cuts you off** or you can tell he's not interested in what you're saying or not listening to you.

70. **He makes fun of your looks or flaws.**

71. **He only talks about himself he never asks you questions.**

72. **When you call him he texts you back because he's around another girl. He has to do this a lot though.**

73. **He keeps forgetting your name**

74. **His profile picture is inappropriate or half nude**. He's lying in bed; he has a towel wrapped around him or he's wearing boxers. Beach gear is fine.

75. **He ignores your calls or text.** He replies days or hours later. Most people have their phone around them 24/7, if they wanted to call you or text you they would, no excuses.

76. **He doesn't want to talk on the phone with you; he only wants to text you.** Some guys are shy at first, but if this guy isn't shy chances are he's a player. Also, after you've met in person the shy guy will talk to you on the phone. Tell him you'd rather talk on the phone and to call you when he's free. If you've already met this guy and he only wants to text, move on.

77. **He doesn't give you a way to contact him**. You only chat with him online. This guy refuses to give you a telephone number, he only chats with you online. He calls you from blocked numbers. You have to wait until he calls you just to hear from him.

78. **He has 2 phones, and he refuses to give you both of the numbers. He has 2 Facebooks, but he won't add you to both.**

79. **Every time you hang out with him women that he knows come up to him, and he doesn't introduce you to them.**

80. **When he's talking to you he doesn't look at you; he's** always looking straight ahead or somewhere else.

81. **You've heard that he's a player.**

82. **When you have a problem with him he runs, avoids you or leaves.** This isn't the type of guy you should take seriously, if you were in a relationship with him he'd run as soon as you argued with him or had a problem. Couples should fix the problem not replace each other. This guy solves his problems by running from them and he solves his relationship problems by replacing people.

83. **He says he isn't looking for a relationship because he's heart broken.** You might feel sorry for him and think you can fix him, but you should just move on. If a guy says he isn't looking for a relationship it means he isn't looking for a relationship with you.

84. **He says he isn't looking for a relationship, but whatever happens happens.** Again this guy isn't looking but he still wants the sex. He's just trying to make you think that you have a chance to change his mind.

85. **He says that he can see himself with you, but not right now**. Any excuse a guy makes not to be with you is rejecting you.

86. **He doesn't want to do anything that you want him to do.** He only wants to do things he wants to do.

87. **He only talks to you when he's bored.**

88. **He leaves conversations with no warning, no apology and he doesn't pick up where he left off.**

89. **He was getting to know you then he vanished for a few days.**

90. He blames all of his problems on the government or his ex or someone else. This guy is the irresponsible type and he will eventually blame you for his problems and actions. He will hit you and blame you for it. He will cheat on you and blame you for it.

91. He doesn't apologize for being late or apologize for anything that he does wrong. This guy has too much pride, he thinks he can do no wrong and he isn't the type to be in a relationship with.

92. When things don't go his way he acts cold and ignores you. He does this to punish you and to get his way. He will pout like a little kid.

93. He's a mama's boy who is constantly hanging around his mom. A man that loves his mom is a good thing, but a man that hangs around his mom 24/7, and can't do anything without her approval is a problem. His mom will seem like his wife instead of his mom, and you'll feel like you're in competition with her for his time. If his mom doesn't approve of you, you're out the door. This guy will always call mom when has a problem with you.

94. When he talks about his past problems he blames everyone else for them. He makes himself the victim in every story he tells you. If you listen closely you'll realize that his stories don't add up.

95. This guy brags about how much money he has, how many cars he has and other things, but you can tell that he's broke or he's lying.

96. He talks bad about little kids, he says they annoy him and he acts rude when they come around. If you want to have kids one day avoid this guy.

97. He treats his pets wrong, *he kicks the dog, or he does other cruel things. Most serial killers hurt animals then they start hurting humans.*

99. He doesn't take care of the kids he already has. If you have kids with him and you break up with him he'll do the same thing to you.

100. He has kids, but he never spends time with them. He blames their mother for him not being in their life. Real dads fight to see their kids; they don't make excuses. That's what the court systems are for. Also, some dads lie on the mom of their kids. She might want him to be a part of the kid's life, but he doesn't want to be. Again, he says this to neglect his responsibilities and to blame someone else for not doing something that he's supposed to do. He will do the same thing if you have kids with him

101. He cheated in his previous relationships. Some people stop cheating and some people don't but if you're looking for a long term serious relationship it's best to find someone who thinks that cheating is wrong.

102. He already has a girlfriend, but he's flirting with you. He will say she's treating him wrong just to get you to talk to him and feel sorry for him.

103. You gave him your number over 3 days ago and he hasn't called you yet. Or it has been over 3 days and he's just now calling you. When a guy is interested in getting to know you he calls you as soon as he gets your number or at least the next day. If it has been over 4 days this guy has too many chicks to keep up with.

104. He hasn't called you in a while, but as soon as he sees you online he calls you or text you. This guy wasn't even thinking about you, he just called you because he saw you online looking for someone else, and he decided he would try to get you in bed again.

105. He asks for your number at an event or outing, and then you see him asking other girls for their numbers. This guy isn't the type you should take seriously.

106. Everything he says seems rehearsed like he's pretending to be Romeo. Some guys are naturally sweet, but this guy uses line after line on you. When he speaks to you he says sweet thing after sweet thing and line after line.

107. When he calls you he speaks to low like he's whispering. Chances are he has another girl.

108. When he calls you, you always hear women in the background even though he says he lives alone.

109. He tells you not to wear lipstick or perfume around him. When he hugs you he removes his jacket or shirt to avoid getting your smell on him. When you kiss him he quickly removes any traces of lip stick. He fixes himself up before he leaves your house or the dating location to remove all evidence of being around another woman. This man is taken.

110. When you're out with him, he constantly leaves to talk on the phone.

111. When you're out with him, he's constantly looking around, and he seems paranoid like he's looking for someone or avoiding someone.

112. He says he just got out of a relationship. Don't be a rebound.

113. He avoids local spots. He always wants to go out of town to hang out. He wants to go to the movies in another city to avoid getting caught. He'll tell you it's better over there.

114. He keeps getting in fights with other men and sometimes it's for a dumb reason.

115. You constantly see scratches on him like he got into a fight with a chick.

116. He keeps talking about another girl and you can tell that he has feelings for her.

117. His stories don't add up. When he tells you something his story doesn't add up, it seems far-fetched, and you know he's' lying

118. He says that women think he's a player, but he's not one.

119. He's into himself. A stuck up guy only has room for one person in his life and that's himself. You'll notice that he always talks about himself, brags about his looks and thinks that all women want him.

120. When he runs into someone he knows he doesn't introduce you to them.

121. He asks for money to come see you or spend time with you.

122. He acts like you have to prove that you're good enough to be with him. He acts like he's too good for you or better than you.

123. He judges you for things he does himself or he judges you or your lifestyle.

124. **He acts like he's famous or someone that he isn't.** For example; he's a waiter, but he acts like he's rich. Or he's a local singer, but he acts like he's a famous superstar. He has a big ego and acts narcissistic. He over exaggerates who is and what he does.

125. **He acts like he's too good for all women.** He will tell you that all the women he has met weren't good enough for him and they were losers or worthless. He will make you feel like you have to prove your worth to him. Usually this man has high unrealistic standards and he doesn't meet his own standards.

126. **He says he isn't looking for just sex, but he keeps trying to have sex with you and rush you to give it up.** Every man that's attracted to you wants to have sex with you. He's lying to try to get you to let your guard down.

127. **His dating profile doesn't add up.** He says he isn't looking for a relationship in one box and in another box he says he can't find Mrs. Right could you be her? His profile says he isn't looking for a relationship but he writes you a long message saying that he really wants to get to know you. If you're looking for a relationship don't date a man that has not looking in his profile.

128. **He bashes women in his online profile,** and acts like all women are the same.

129. **His dating profile is full of unrealistic expectations** or he's looking for things that he doesn't have himself. For example; he's only looking for Barbie look alike even though he's average Joe. Or he's only looking for women with a college degree even though his highest education is high school. He's only looking for intelligent woman, but he can't spell simple words.

130. **He tries to keep you from dating other men even though he hasn't claimed you, and he's still dating other women or looking for other women.**

131. **He says he's never had a serious relationship, and he's over 35.**

132. **He says he doesn't have sex or anything because he's in the church, but he keeps trying to have sex with you.**

133. **He preaches to you about your sins and things you shouldn't be doing, but he's sinning too.** He tells you that you need to come to church. He acts like you're the sinner and he's the saint. He even tries to have sex with you. This guy is a hypocrite, and he's usually a leader, a minister or a member of a church.

134. **When he's around his friends or other people he treats you differently or he's rude to you.**

135. **He's in and out of jail. He's a trouble maker, he's always getting into trouble or he makes his money illegally.**

136. **He blames you for things that he does wrong.** Move on because this will get worse. Never blame yourself for someone else's actions. You can only control your actions not his actions.

140. **He acts like he's in love with you but he doesn't even know your full name yet or anything about you.** Chances are it's just lust.

141. **He makes last minute plans.** Don't accept last minute plans. This guy never makes plans in advance they're always at the last minute.

142. He always talks to you on the phone for a few minutes then he has to go. When a guy is into you he'll talk to you on the phone for hours sometimes or at least listen to you. If he's always rushing you off the phone he's not into you.

143. He only has one picture or he refuses to send you any pictures. Make sure this guy is really the guy in his profile picture because people do make fake pages. Tell him to send you a picture that isn't online or web cam with you.

144. He's in town temporarily. This guy is on vacation; he's traveling for business or just visiting a relative. He might be hot, but he's leaving soon so don't get involved with him. Some men travel for business and they have women all over the place.

145. He sent you a few nice emails then he disappeared. If a guy is interested in getting to know you he won't disappear. This guy wasn't that interested in you if he has already left after a few emails. Don't write him or chase him, if he wanted you he would have kept in contact. If you still see him online he's looking for someone else. However, he might write you again if he doesn't find anyone else, but you should ignore him. Never let a man come and go as he pleases. Also, don't think that you did something wrong. Some men stop writing because they're looking for someone easier, and some men stop writing because they don't think you're the one. Don't take it personal just realize that he isn't the one, and be happy that he only wasted a few days of your time instead of months or years.

146. He is making you chase him. You just met this guy and he's already making you do all of the work to keep things going.

147. He invites you to things or places that he's already at. He asks you to join him at a bar or an event that he's already at. He does this because he has already scoped out the chicks there and he didn't find anyone to take home or talk to. So, he calls you to come over and give him some company etch.

QUICK QUIZ

1. You're looking for a relationship, and a hot guy messages you online. He says he really wants to get to know you and you're the prettiest girl on the website. When you click his profile he seems like the perfect guy for you, but his profile says he's not looking for anything serious.

Do you move on or do you write him back because he's so hot?

Move on, he's not looking for a relationship he's just looking for sex. Don't chase him and try to change his mind.

2. You've been getting to know this guy for a few days. He sends you good morning text. He makes you smile and he keeps giving you compliments. You haven't been on a date with him yet. Then one day he asks you if he can come over and cuddle with you.

Do you say yes because you like him? Or do you tell him that you'd rather meet somewhere else?

Meet somewhere else for the first 5 dates. He should be taking you out or doing something interesting outside of the house. A real date. If he doesn't want to take you on real dates cut him off.

3. He keeps asking you to send him sexy pictures of you, he keeps talking about sex, and he's barely asking you real questions.

Do you send him the pictures or do you stop talking to him?

Cut him off.

4. He acts really interested in you. Then he vanishes for a couple of days then pops back up and starts acting interested again.

Do you reply to him because you like him and he's hot or do you ignore his calls and text?

Ignore him. If you reply you're going to get stuck with a guy that blows hot and cold, uses you and goes in and out of your life as he pleases.

5. He wants to meet you for Dinner at your favorite restaurant on Saturday night. But on Friday night he asks if you can meet him at a bar for drinks instead?

Do you say yes or do you decline his offer?

Decline his offer. A bar isn't a real date and you shouldn't drink on dates with guys you don't know. If he's into you he'll stick with the current plans. If he was just trying to get laid he won't offer you anything else.

6. You're having a lovely dinner with him at a nice restaurant. Then the waitress accidentally spills a little bit of his drink on the table as she is handing it to him. He yells at her, criticizes her and keeps being rude to her even though she keeps apologizing.

Do you ignore it because it has nothing to do with you or do you cut him off?

Cut him off. This is exactly how he will treat you when he gets mad at you. He has no respect for women, especially women who he thinks is beneath him.

7. He showed up 1 hour late without calling you on the first date, and the second date he didn't show up at all, he just stood you up. Now he wants you to meet him on Friday to make it up to you.

Do you give him another chance or do you cut him off?

Cut him off. This guy only sees you as an option. Someone that will just wait around for him.

8. You gave him your number 1 week ago and he's just now calling you.

Do you try to get to know him or do you cut him off?

Cut him off. This guy has way too many chicks already. If he was into you he would have called you the same day or next day. A week is ridiculous.

9. He took you on 2 real dates and he tells you to call him when you get home. He doesn't talk about sex, he doesn't rush you to have sex and he keeps asking you questions about your life, your goals and your dreams. He talks to you every day and he keeps the conversations going. He tells you all kinds of things about himself. You haven't been in an argument with him and you've never seen him mad or upset about anything?

Do you know this guy well enough to sleep with him? Yes, or No?

No, you haven't seen all sides of him. You like him because you've only seen the good stuff. Wait until he connects with you emotionally and you get to know him better (his good and bad side)

10. This guy wrote you a few nice emails and then he disappeared. You like him so far and you want to keep chatting with him.

Do you email him again or do you just forget about him?

Forget about him. If he's already running after a few emails he isn't the one for you. Also, you've only seen his good side so you really don't know this guy yet anyway. Be happy that he only wasted a few days instead of months or years. Never chase a guy!

11. This guy was texting you for a few days, but he stopped texting you, and you still see him online.

Do you text him first or do you wait for him to text you first?

You might be interested in this guy, but you shouldn't text him first. A guy that's interested in you will text you again, but don't respond if it has been over 3 days OR if you've seen him online since then.

12. This hot guy asks you if you can show him around town. He says he's in town for business and he'd love to get to know you.

Do you show him around town or do you decline his offer?

Decline his offer. Chances are he's looking for a fling.

13. This guy wants you to come over to his house for dinner. He wants to cook for you on the first date.

Do you accept his invitation or do you decline?

This is a sweet idea, but you don't know this guy well enough to be going to his house. First dates should be out in public. Also, this guy could be a player who's trying to get you to come to his house. Never go to a guy's house for the first 5 dates no matter how sweet his plans sound. Always remember that a player will say or do anything to get you to come to their house so they can get laid.

14. This guy wants you to drive to see him. He lives in another county.

Do you drive to see him or do you meet him half way?

Real men drive to see you, but some modern day men want to meet half way. If a guy wants you to drive to see him, and he refuses to meet you half way decline his offer. Also, if this guy has a problem with driving to see you now you shouldn't be in a long distance relationship with him. Also if you hate driving long distances you shouldn't be in a long distance relationship. Don't get into something that you know won't work out. If you don't want to drive hours to see him, and he doesn't want to drive hours to see you it won't work. Some men are used to women chasing after them and driving hours just to see them. Don't do what a man is supposed to do.

15. This guy wants you to go on a date with him.

Do you let him pick you up or do you meet him at the dating location?

Meet him at the dating location. So, the date will end at the dating location instead of at your house. This also keeps you from drinking too much because you have to drive yourself home, and it keeps him from pressuring you to let him in when he drops you off.

16. The guy you just met sends you a picture of his penis.

Do you compliment him; do you tell him not to send those kinds of pictures or do you cut him off?

Cut him off, this guy doesn't respect you and he's just looking for sex. If he sent it to you, chances are he sends it to other women too, and who wants a boyfriend like that?

17. **You just met this guy and he keeps talking about sex, talking about how sexy you are and the things he would do to you.**

Do you join in? Do you flirt back or do you cut him off?

If you join in your signing up for 'sex only'. If you're looking for a relationship cut him off.

18. **You just met this guy and he's already acting like you're not good enough for him and he acts like you have to prove that you're good enough for him. He acts like he's too good for you or he acts like he's better than you, and you feel like he's asking you to prove your worth to him.**

Do you prove yourself to him or do you cut him off?

Cut him off. This guy is already putting himself above you and acting like you're not good enough. Move on because he'll always act like this and you'll be stuck chasing a guy who'll never think you're good enough. Never stay with someone that acts like they're better than you or with someone that acts like you're not good enough.

19. **You meet this cute guy at the club, he gives you a bunch of compliments and you give him your number. He calls you after the club and wants you to come over to his place.**

Do you go or do you decline his offer?

Decline. This guy is looking for someone to have sex with right now. If he really wants to get to know you he'll call you the next day or so and set up a real date. If he wants to get breakfast after the club that's fine just meet him there and don't go home with him afterward unless you want to be in the sex only zone.

20. **You've been on over 5 real dates with him. He is opening up to you emotionally, asking you real questions and spending a lot of time getting to know you. He doesn't vanish, he talks to you on the phone and you really like him. Now, he wants you to come over to his house to watch a movie.**

Do you decline his offer? Do you watch the movie but don't have sex with him? Do you watch the movie and have sex afterward?

Since you've been on 5 real dates it's okay to go over. Go over, but don't have sex with him yet. Wait until he wants to take things to the next level. (Be exclusive) If he tries to have sex with you tell him that you don't have sex unless you're in an exclusive relationship. If you have sex with him without a commitment you're telling him that you're okay with no strings attached sex. If he's into you he'll be exclusive if not he'll vanish, but at least you won't get used for sex. If you have sex with him without a commitment, why should he commit to you?

21. **The guy drops you off and asks if he can come into your house to use the restroom.**

Do you let him in or do you tell him to hold it?

Tell him to hold it. If he had to use the restroom that bad he would have used it at the dating location. Don't fall for that line he just wants to come inside. Also, if you don't know him yet it's dangerous to let him in.

22. You just met this guy and he's all over you. He's touching you all over and trying to feel on you. He's even trying to kiss you.

Do you let him do it because he's hot or do you cut him off?

Cut him off. Decent guys don't grope you when you first meet them. If he's groping you on the first date he's trying to get laid. Big player sign.

23. You've been talking and dancing with a guy at the club all night. You exchange numbers and he says he wants you to come over and chill and he'll take you home.

Do you leave with him because he's hot or do you decline his offer?

Decline. This guy just wants to get laid. Never leave the club or a party with a stranger; I don't care how hot he is. It's dangerous and it makes you look easy.

If you got all 23 correct CONGRATS your chances of getting played are slim to none. If you got a few wrong, go back over this guide again so you won't get played.

Basically, no matter how much you like the guy you can't ignore these signs.

Also, you should still be dating other men. If he hasn't claimed you, you should still be dating. Men are competitors if they see you dating other men they will try to claim you before anyone else can. If they think they already have you wrapped around their finger they won't feel the need to claim you. Single women shouldn't sleep around, but they should date around until they find a man that wants them for more than just sex. Date around don't sleep around. No man wants to claim a woman that sleeps around. The more men you date the better your chances of finding Mr. Right.

Cut them off before they get a chance to play you.

Use common sense and logic to make your decisions.

SIGNS HE'S PLAYING YOU OR HE'S NOT INTO YOU

80 SIGNS HE'S A PLAYER, CHEATER OR A JERK

If he does 5 or more of the things below he's definitely NOT into you or he's playing games.

1. A player will say anything to get you to like them, but they won't do anything for you. Basically, they will tell you a lot of things, but they won't back it up. Always go by their actions and not their words.

2. A player will act really interested in you, but they will never commit to you or take things to the next level. He will act like he's your boyfriend, but he won't claim you or commit to you.

3. A player will blow hot and cold on you. Sometimes they'll act interested in you and sometimes they'll ignore you and act like you don't exist. They will go in and out of your life.

4. They will blame you for everything that they do wrong. If they hit you they blame you for making them do it. If they cheat on you they blame you for why they cheated. Players always find a way to put everything on you and make it seem like it's your fault.

5. Players will lie about everything, because they want to keep you around. You'll notice that their lies and excuses are dumb and they don't make sense. When you catch them lying they make it seem like you're overreacting or they deny it.

6. Players will confuse you. They will say that they love, but they will keep disrespecting you, cheating on you and beating you. You will be confused because they will act lovey dovey one day and the next day they will act like a totally different person. Since you're in love with their good side you try to put up with their bad side.

7. Players will say they don't want a relationship, but they will treat you like they're your girlfriend. They do this because they know you'll leave if they don't show you some affection. He can act like he's your boyfriend but if he never commits to you he's your friend with benefits and he thinks you're just his Mrs. RIGHT now.

8. Players will act like you're not good enough to be their girlfriend. You will try to prove that you can be their girlfriend you will show them a lot of love and always be there for them. But no matter what you do, they never commit to you because they're not into you.

9. Players will say that they love you, but they can't be with you right now. When you love someone you'd do anything to be with them right now. They don't think you're the one so they use this line to lead you on.

10. Players will act like they love you in private, but in public they'll treat you like you're just a friend. They don't want anyone to know they're dating you and they're trying to keep it a secret.

11. Players won't introduce you to their parents.

12. Players won't send you any messages that everyone can read. They always send IM'S, DM'S or emails. They never show you love in front of other people.

13. Players don't stay the night or cuddle with you after sex. They leave as soon as sex is over.

14. Players will flirt with other women in front of you.

15. Players won't take care of your emotional needs. They'll only take care of your sexual needs.

16. You're getting played if you feel used and you feel as if they don't care about you.

17. Players won't try to get to know you. You'll feel like you're always asking them questions, but they never ask you questions.

18. Players will act one-sided. They will look through your phone, emails and purse, but if you try to look through their stuff they'll get mad at you. They can go out with their friends, but they don't want you to go out with your friends.

19. Players take their phone everywhere with them. They keep it on silent, face down or vibrate and they NEVER leave their phone around you.

20. Players don't add you to their Facebook, twitter or other social sites because they're hiding things from you.

21. Players are always adding new numbers to their phone, and they have weird names in their phone

22. Players always have their phone when they're around you, but when they're away from you they act like they never have it. They act like they didn't get your call or text or email. Or they act like they sent you a text or called you, but your phone must be broken. Or they'll say that they called you, but they kept getting your voice-mail.

23. Players use the same excuse for a lot of things. Every time they do something they give you that same excuse.

24. Players get REALLY mad at you when you question them. They ACT really mad because they're trying to get you to back down and they're guilty. Some girls stop asking questions because they're afraid of how mad their man will get.

25. Players will get mad at you then vanish for days without contacting you.

26. Players vanish for long periods of time without contacting you, and when they vanish they ignore your phone calls and text.

27. Players will vanish then blame you for not calling them. Even though you probably did call, but they ignored you. They'll say things like "Why didn't you call me?" and when you tell them that you DID call them they will act like they didn't get your call or text.

28. Players make up excuses for not being with you or spending time with you. They're just not into you.

29. Players hurt you, then apologize then hurt you all over again. This keeps going until you realize that they're not going to change and you LEAVE them.

30. Players make you do all the calling, texting, planning and fighting. They only call you or text you FIRST when they want to come over or they want something from you. Other than that you have to initiate all of the contact.

31. Players won't seem interested in conversations about you or your life. They only act interested in the conversation if it's something about them or something they want.

32. Players are never there when you really need them or for emotional support. They act like they don't care about you when you're sad, when you cry or when you're sick.

33. Players don't spend Holidays with you, and they don't buy you gifts on your birthday, Valentine's Day or any other special days.

34. Players that are using you as a booty call will only hang around with you at night, AND you will never hang out with them during the day time.

35. Players that are using you as a booty call will only come over late at night, after the club or when they're drunk.

36. Players will want to keep the relationship a secret. They will say I don't want anyone in our business so let's keep it a secret.

37. Players will try to talk to you even though they already have a girlfriend. They will tell you that they're fixing to break up with her or divorce her because she's treating them wrong or some other sob story. The truth is they're not leaving her they just want to have their cake and eat it too, AND their wife or girlfriend might not be the bitch he claims she is. The wife or girlfriend might be sweet and unaware that her man is cheating on her. If he does it to her chances are he'll do it to you.

38. Players will give you an excuse for not being with you. Any excuse someone gives you not to be with you is rejecting you. However, he'll still keep you around for sex.

39. Players will change right after you have sex with them BECAUSE sex is all they came for in the first place.

40. When you call him he texts you back instead of answering the phone. Basically, he's around another female and he can't answer the phone when she's around. He has to do this a lot though.

41. He disappears at night time. When night time rolls around you can't get a hold of him or he has other times that he vanishes.

42. You can never get a hold of him. You always get his voice mail when you call. So, you have to wait until he calls you.

43. He has a home phone and a cell phone, but he refuses to give you both of the numbers.

44. He doesn't tell you anything about himself or his personal life. Basically he keeps everything about himself a secret.

45. You don't know where he stays or you've never been to his house.

46. When he answers the phone around you he changes his voice into the "Oh shit I'm busted" voice. He acts strange when he answers it and keeps looking at you.

47. He goes into another room to answer the phone. Whispering on phone calls.

48. When he answers the phone in front of you he gives the other person 1 or 2 word answers and rushes them off the phone.

49. When you catch him texting someone he makes sure he keeps the phone screen out of your view. The closer you get to him the more he moves the phone away from you.

50. He never takes you on Romantic dates. Nice dates that couples go on not just to grab something to eat or meet up at a bar or club.

51. Your name in his phone isn't your real name or your pet name. It's under a guy's name or some other crazy name or initials.

52. They constantly delete their web history, text, and call logs.

53. He constantly accuses you of doing bad things even though you haven't given him a reason not to trust you. Chances are he's doing those things.

54. He flakes on you, stands you up. He makes plans with you at the last minute and always cancels things at the last minute. Basically, you're just one of his options.

55. He's never at home. He always finds a reason to leave the house OR he always finds a reason to not come home.

56. All of his friends are players and he hangs out with them more than he hangs out with you. And he uses one of his player friends as his alibi. Like I was with Matt call him and ask him.

57. Your friends and family are trying to warn you about him.

58. Unknown numbers call his phone and when you answer it they hang up on you. Chances are the other woman knows about you and she hangs up when you answer.

59. His phone rings nonstop, but he never answers it in front of you. However, he might send them a quick text message if they keep calling him. Someone will be blowing his phone up, but he will just text them back to get them to stop calling.

60. He used to have a lot of time for you, but now he acts like he has ZERO time for you. He keeps saying that he's busy or going to be busy. However, he does make time for the things that he wants to do.

61. He will never call just to check on you and see how you're doing. He only calls when he wants to meet up come over or when he wants something.

62. He lies to the person he's talking to on the phone. He tells them he's doing something that he isn't doing or he tells them he's with someone that he isn't with. Then he lies to you about who he was talking to.

63. They ask you to come over to their house for the first date/ meet up or they want to come to your house. They just want to get laid and skip the dating stage.

64. They try to get you drunk on the first few dates so they can try to get laid.

65. He doesn't want to kiss you during sex or he used to kiss you, but he doesn't kiss you anymore or you know he likes to kiss but he refuses to kiss you.

66. When you come around he rushes off of phone calls or logs off of the computer.

67. He lives with you, eats your food, drives your car, has sex with you and spends your money, but he doesn't claim you.

68. If he can fuck you ALL night, but he doesn't make time to call and talk to you for a FEW MINUTES you know what time is.

69. He calls you boo or bae in text or in private, but in public he acts like you're just a friend.

70. He ignores you he barely calls you during the weekdays, but when it's close to the weekend he blows your phone up because he wants to meet up or hook up.

71. He only text/calls you during the daytime. At night time he ignores you and you can't get a hold of him.

72. He never text you first, if you don't text him first you won't hear from him.

73. You just met him and he's already calling you boo or bae. Or he calls you his babe, honey or boo in private, but in public he acts like you're just a friend or he says you're just a friend.

74. You're in a relationship with him but he calls you OOMF instead of mentioning your @name.

75. If you write on his Facebook Wall he erases it or ignores it. He un-tags himself from your pictures. He ignores your mentions and text you instead of replying. He keeps tweeting and updating his Facebook but he hasn't text you back.

76. He text you, then you call him as soon as you get his text and he ignores your call. This has to happen a lot though.

77. He only hits you up when he's in town. He wants someone to hook up with when he's in town.

77. He only talks to you in private, in emails or in IMS. He never talks to you in public or around someone he knows.

78. How he treats you in public is way different from how he treats you in private. This guy is trying to keep you a secret.

79. When you catch him doing something wrong he tries to flip the script and blame you for doing the same thing or blame you for doing something wrong. You look through his phone and see text messages from him to other women. He gets mad at you for looking through his phone and tries to make you seem like the bad guy. Don't fall for this game, he's just trying to change the subject, and put the blame on you.

80. When you catch him cheating he blames you for why he's cheating on you. He blames you for everything he does wrong.

Below are a few games that players play. DON'T play these games just use them as a learning tool

1. Be good in bed, no be excellent. Make them addicted to your sex.
2. Keep your phone on silent in your pocket or purse. Don't answer it or text in front of them. Out of sight, out of mind
3. Once someone is interested in you only call them when you need something. Let them do the rest of the texting and calling. Keep them chasing you.
4. . Tell them you're not looking for a relationship, but tell them that you really want to get to know them and whatever happens happens. They will think that they can be the girl that will change your mind, but they can't blame you later because you told them you weren't looking.
5. Make them feel special and like they're the only one you like whenever you see them. If you make them feel special they'll want to hang around you all the time, but barely give them any of your time.
6. Make their dreams come true: Find out what they're looking for in a man or woman and become that. When you meet them ask them what they're looking for and become that.

   7. Make your words flow like music to their ears. Be smooth but don't be too obvious. Don't use cookie cutter pickup lines. Tell them what they want to hear, make them fall in love with you.

   8. You can't act desperate or too stuck up. Be cocky at the right times, be funny and easy going. Smile a lot.

   9. You must be confident. Low self-esteem won't get you far.

10. You have to have the "I don't give a fuck attitude". If you care about hurting people's feelings, you can't play. Act like you care sometimes and other times act like you don't care. This will confuse them and you'll be a mystery to them. When you act like you don't care they'll think that they did something wrong and try to fix it.

11. Never give them what they want. This will keep them chasing you.

12. When things don't go your way act cold and distant. They'll chase after you and give you what you want because they want your attention again. Do this every time they act up.

13. Pretend to care about them sometimes so they'll feel special and keep giving you what you want.

14. Make them feel like they're not good enough. They'll keep trying to prove that they're good enough for you and do everything they can to get you, but never let them get you. After all you're not into them, but you do like what they're giving you.

15. Get them in bed as soon as possible

16. When you're around them act like you're in love with them, but when you're in public or away from them act like they're just a friend or you don't know them like that. Treat her like a girlfriend in private and a friend in public. This will confuse them, but since they love the attention they get from you and the sex they'll stick around.

17. Don't hang around after sex.

18. Avoid her on holidays or special occasions. You don't want her to get the wrong idea.

19. If she tells you she has feelings for you, make up some kind of an excuse for not wanting to commit to her so you can keep her around. Like you're not ready or your heart is broken or you're bad for her. If she keeps bringing up relationships vanish.

20. Cuddle with her before sex but not after sex. Cuddling before sex will get her in the mood so you can get laid.

21. Only hang out at your place or hers. Never take her on real dates because she might get the wrong

idea and think you're dating her. Plus, you don't like her like that. If you do hang out, make sure it's not a real date. Group dates, Movie night, bars or fast food is best. Real dates are for chicks you want to impress and wife.

22. Get her drunk on the first few dates so she can loosen up and you can take advantage of her drunkenness

23. Have the first few dates at your house. Ask her to come over and chill, or have a drink or cook for her. Dates at your house put you closer to the bedroom so you can get laid.

24. Blame them for everything that you do wrong. They will think it's their fault and that they must have did something wrong for you to treat them like that. So, they will behave better, show you more love and try to please you. They will also try to fix things so you won't do it again. However, nothing they do will stop you from doing it again because it has NOTHING to do with them, they just happen to be in love with a shitty person like you. One day you'll change, but not today. They can't change you, you have to change yourself but they'll waste their time trying to change you anyway.

25. Pick a girl that's really into you, a girl with low self-esteem, a lonely girl that will do anything to be with you. Pick a desperate girl that is practically throwing herself at you, and worshiping you like you're a King. Girls with low self-esteem will let you get away with everything and let you walk all over them.

26. When you're outside of her house say anything you can to get inside her home. You have to use the restroom, you're thirsty, and you just want to sober up. Say something that will make her feel sorry for you and let you in.

27. Tell her you forgot something at your house and you need to go get it really fast. Try to get her to come inside. Say anything to get her to come into your house. Show her your fish, your movies, anything.

If he says he's too drunk to drive home. Tell him you'll take him home. If you followed the steps above, you should be sober. Take him home and just drop him off. When you drop him off don't go inside just stay in your car. Always remember that a player's goal is to get you in bed ASAP and if you don't want to get played you can't fall for his sneaky games.

When your feelings get hurt players and cheaters only feel bad for you temporarily. Their needs come first at ALL times.

If you spot games just move on. Don't fall in love with WORDS fall in love with ACTIONS. Take things SLOW, because players like to rush. The longer you wait to have sex the more players you can get rid of. Be their friend first so you can see their personality and see if they're really COMPATIBLE with you.

QUICK QUIZ

1. Your 'friend with benefits' says he can't be with you because his heart is broken, and he can't trust anyone.

Do you feel sorry for him and stick around or do you realize that he's rejecting you and move on?

Realize that he's rejecting you and move on. He only wants sex from you.

2. You've been sleeping with a guy for over 6 months, he hasn't claimed you, and he hasn't introduced you to his parents.

Do you just wait for him to ask you out or do you talk to him about where things are going?

Talk to him about where things are going because chances are this guy doesn't think you're the one. If he makes up an excuse to not be with you move on. Don't be afraid to tell him how you feel. The longer you wait the more time you'll waste. If you're afraid to tell him face to face, text it or write him an email and hit send before you chicken out. If you're sleeping with this guy, you have the right to know where you stand with him, and you should want to know.

3. He asks you what you look for in a guy (qualities and characteristics)

Do you tell him everything you're looking for in a guy or do you tell him that you don't have a certain type of guy you just get to know people, and see if they're compatible with you?

Tell him you're looking for a relationship, but don't tell him everything you look for in a guy. If you tell a player you're looking for a funny guy he will become a funny guy. If you tell him you're looking for a smart guy he will act smart even if he isn't smart. Simply because he wants you to like him.

I prefer to get to know people and see if they have the qualities that I'm looking for. Instead of telling someone what I'm looking for and have them purposely become that just to get/keep me interested.

4. This guy never text you first unless he wants to meet up with you or come over.

Do you cut him off or move on?

Cut him off. You're just his booty call or friend with benefits. He only text you first when he wants to make plans to have sex. The rest of the time you have to text him first.

5. This guy doesn't make time to call you, but he makes time to have sex with you. He's too busy to call you, but he's not too busy to have sex or things he wants to do.

Do you cut him off or do you realize that he's just using you for sex?

Cut him off. He's interested in your body not you. It takes a few minutes to call you and a few seconds to text you. If he can make time to have sex with you he can make time to call/text you, he just makes time for what he wants to do.

6. This guy is never there for you emotionally. He doesn't take you on dates and he's never there for you when you have a problem. He never calls you just to check on you. You feel like he's using you for sex.

Do you stick around and try to make him love you or do you move on because you know he's just using you for sex.

Follow your instincts. You feel used because he is using you. You feel used because he's never there for you and you know he doesn't care about you. He pretends to like you sometimes because he wants to get you in bed.

7. He flirts with other women in front of you. He keeps cheating on you, and hurting you. Then he apologizes, says he loves you and says he wants to marry you one day.

Do you believe that he's in love with you or do you realize that he doesn't love you and he's just playing you?

He's not in love with you and he's a cheater, move on. Do you want to spend the rest of your life with a guy that keeps cheating on you? Is that the type of men you want to have a family with? Also, he's putting your health at risk.

8. This guy cuddles with you before sex and watches movies with you. Then he has sex with you and leaves as soon as sex is over or he makes you leave. He acts like your boyfriend when you're alone with him, but he refuses to commit to you. He says he wants to be with you, but not right now.

Do you wait for him and try to prove that you're good enough to be his girlfriend or do you cut him off?

Cut him off. When a guy loves you he claims you before anyone else can. ANY EXCUSE SOMEONE MAKES NOT TO BE WITH YOU IS REJECTING YOU. He doesn't think you're the one.

9. This guy was nice at first, but right after sex he changed. After you have sex with him he starts ignoring you or acting cold/distant.

Do you chase him and try to make him like you again or do you realize that he was just looking for sex and move on?

You thought he was nice because you only knew the good stuff about him. Move on because he only wanted sex from you. Connect with a guy emotionally before you connect with him physically, and get to know all sides of him. Don't give him what he wants until he's giving you what you need. It's best to wait until he claims you. If he doesn't think you're good enough to claim don't sleep with him.

10. Sometimes he ignores your text and sometimes he responds. When he responds he doesn't keep the conversation going.

Do you keep texting him or do you realize that he's not into you?

He's not into you. He only acts interested in you when he wants something. When he doesn't want anything from you he ignores you.

11. He stopped talking to you months ago, but now he's hitting you up again. You tried to text/call him before but he ignored you. He asks you for your number, and he makes up an excuse for why he stopped talking to you. He says he lost your number, got a new phone or some other excuse.

Do you give him another chance or do you ignore him?

Ignore him. He didn't lose your number he just lost interest in you, but now that he's lonely or horny he's hitting you up again. If you give him another chance he's going to go in and out of your life as he pleases. Chances are the girl he left you for didn't work out and he needs a replacement.

13. You've been seeing this guy for over a year, you haven't met his parents yet, and he doesn't claim you.

Do you keep seeing him or do you cut him off?

Cut him off. He doesn't think you're the one.

14. This guy acts like your boyfriend in private, but he refuses to claim you and he introduces you as a friend. He acts like he loves you in private, but in public he acts like you're just a friend to him.

Do you keep seeing him or do you realize that he's not into you?

Realize he's not into you. A guy that's into you will be happy to claim you. A guy doesn't want to be 'just friends' with someone he's in love with."

15. Every time you ask him a question, he answers it, but he doesn't ask you a question back.

Do you keep asking him questions or do you realize that he's not into you?

He's not into you, and he doesn't ask you questions because he doesn't want to get to know you.

16. This guy goes in and out of your life. He keeps vanishing for days at a time, and he ignores you a lot. He always has an excuse for why he's ignoring you. He claims to be busy.

Do you cut him off or do you chase him and try to make him love you?

Cut him off, you're just an option to him. You're sharing him with other women. He pops back up when it's your turn.

17. This guy never answers your phone calls, but he calls you at his own times. You can never get a hold of him. Everything is on his schedule.

Do you stick around or do you realize that he's playing games?

If he only calls you when he wants to and he never answers your phone calls he's playing games.

18. You just met this guy and you've already caught him lying about a dozen things.

Do you cut him off or do you give him a chance anyway?

Cut him off. If you give a liar a chance, he will mess up your life. If he's already lying about a dozen things, things will get worse. Trust is an important part of a relationship.

19. This guy never takes you out. He only wants to hang out at your house or his house, and he doesn't stick around to cuddle with you after sex.

Do you keep seeing him or do you realize that he's just using you for sex?

Realize that he's just using you for sex.

20. This guy doesn't spend time with you on Holidays or your birthday. He avoids you on those days. He makes up an excuse for not being available that day or he sends you a text. Nothing to make you feel special.

Do you keep seeing this guy or do you realize that he only wants sex from you?

He only wants sex. When a guy is into you he spends time with you on Holidays even if he can't afford to buy you a gift.

21. He acts jealous and he tries to stop you from dating other guys, but he doesn't want to commit to you.

Do you think he's jealous because he's in love with you or do you think he's jealous because he doesn't want to share you sexually?

He just doesn't' want you to sleep with anyone else. If he was in love with you he'd claim you before another guy could.

22. This guy only wants to hang out with you at bars and clubs. He never takes you on real dates, and he doesn't claim you.

Do you keep seeing him or do you realize that he isn't in to you?

Realize that he isn't into you

23. This guy is always calling you late at night asking you if he can come over.

Do you let him come over or do you realize that he's just making a booty call?

He's using you for sex. You're his booty call

24. This guy doesn't try to get to know you, he doesn't take you on real dates, and he never text you first unless he's asking you to come over.

Do you keep seeing him or do you realize that he's using you?

He doesn't want to get to know you he's just using you.

25. Your boyfriend broke up with you last week, but he's still trying to have sex with you.

Do you have sex with him or do you realize that he's just trying to have his cake and eat it too?

He's just trying to keep the benefits. Basically, he wants to go from commitment to no strings attached sex. Have his cake and eat it too.

26. This guy ignored you before, but now he's saying that he misses you.

Do you give him another chance or do you realize that he's just trying to get in your pants?

He ignored you before because he replaced you and lost interest in you, but now he's horny and he thinks you'll give him some.

27. You catch him cheating on you. You looked through his phone and saw flirty text from him to other women. He gets mad at you and says that you had no right to look through his phone.

Do you feel bad for looking through his phone or do you realize that he's just trying to turn things around on you?

It doesn't matter how you found out about his cheating. What matters is that he was cheating on you. If he wasn't cheating, you would not have found anything in his phone. Never let a man blame you for the things that he does wrong.

If this guide made you realize that you're being played. Realize that he's Mr. Wrong and one day you will find Mr. Right.

If you enjoyed this guide, please leave Feed Back and share it with your girlfriends.

The paperback version of this book can be written in and it's great for workshops and lectures.

If you don't love yourself, you'll let people get away with things that you KNOW aren't right.

Read my book "35 STEPS TO LOVING YOURSELF" and start loving yourself today.

Now that you know your worth get the "I love me, and I know my worth" wristband from my website SlimPhatty.com or on Amazon.com This wristband will remind you 24/7 to remember your worth. It comes in red, pink or black with my logo to remind you of my words to you.

If you need help letting, go of someone you love read my book '25 Steps to Letting Go OF Someone You love'

Can you handle rejection? Learn how by reading '12 Steps to Learning How to Handle Rejection'

Need help getting back on your feet? 'Read 29 Steps to Getting Back On Your Feet"

Dating Guide for Single Women has tons of things you should know about modern day dating, and it includes topics to build your self-esteem and self- worth. It also includes Commitment, the different types of players and friends with benefits information.

Subscribe to me on YouTube for free helpful videos.

"Some people are breaking their back for a person that is only breaking their heart."

Made in the USA
Coppell, TX
30 May 2020